THAI
COOKING

To Sue, Arthur, Laurie, Walter and Robby who ate unstintingly.

Thanks to the students at the California Culinary Academy; Michael Bauer; Karen Frerichs; Carol Hacker; Janet Hazen; Gibson Scheid; Jan and Bill Stein; and to Kelly for her wonderful recipes.

Joyce Oudkerk Pool

• FOODS OF THE WORLD •

THAI
COOKING

Kelly Simon

Photography by Joyce Oudkerk Pool

LITTLE BROWN
AND COMPANY
BOSTON • TORONTO • LONDON

A Little, Brown book

A Kevin Weldon Production
Weldon Publishing is
a division of Kevin Weldon & Associates Pty Limited
Level 5, 70 George Street, Sydney, Australia

This edition first published in 1993

ISBN: 0-316-90605-0
A CIP catalogue record for this book
is available from the British Library

Edited by Patricia Connell and Alice Scott
Food stylist: Daniel Bowe
Printed in Singapore by Kyodo Printing Co (S'pore) Pte Ltd

Little, Brown and Company (UK) Ltd
165 Great Dover Street
London SE1 4YA

CONTENTS

INTRODUCTION

Thai meals usually consist of three to five main dishes, each bearing a distinct flavour—salty, sweet, hot, sour and bland. The bland element is usually steamed rice, an essential part of a Thai meal. A typical dinner might comprise some kind of curry, a soup, a vegetable dish served together with steamed rice, and a *yam* or salad. The meal is accompanied by potent and pungent sauces—*nam priks*, for instance—and is followed by dessert.

Soup, almost always accompanied by steamed rice, is not a separate course; it is served in a tureen along with the rest of the meal. Diners help themselves. Soup is also eaten at any time during the day. The meal is served at a low table, the diners seated on cushions around it. There is no set course sequence; dishes are served simultaneously, with guests helping themselves as they wish.

Thai food is a combination of many cuisines, most notably those of China and India, though it is very distinct from them. Whereas soy sauce and cornflour are ubiquitous in China, they are less common in Thai recipes. Soy sauce is generally replaced by fish sauce (*nam pla*), a potent amber-coloured liquid made from fermented anchovies.

The preparation of Thai meals intimidates some cooks because many of the recipes call for seasoning pastes, which are fairly time-consuming to make. In cities housing large Asian populations, red, green and orange curry pastes (see pages 8, 9 and 10) are available in plastic containers at reasonable prices. Even in Thailand many people have abandoned the practice of making their own curry pastes and are buying them commercially, though they are not as complex or as intense as those made from scratch. Pounding the ingredients in a mortar yields the finest, most authentic product but it is a time-consuming process; you will probably prefer to use a mini-food processor, as I suggest in the recipes. The quantities used in these recipes are not sufficient for a full-size processor.

A cautionary word: never try to pulverise dried galangal root (*kha, ka, laos*) in your spice grinder or processor. It must be soaked first.

You will be amazed at the rich harvest of condiments you can glean from a market that caters to an Asian clientele. Such specialties as rice, wheat, egg, scallop and prawn noodles; dry and wet spice mixes; bottled table sauces; not to mention satay sauces, Mussaman curry pastes, salted prawns (*kapi*), coconut milk and cream, salty-sour *tom yum* cubes and pastes, tamarind soup bases and pastes can be found at prices far less than what it would cost to prepare them at home.

It simplifies matters enormously to make up a batch of basic pastes and sauces in advance. In addition to the red, green and orange curry pastes mentioned above, chilli-garlic sauce (page 17), roasted curry paste (page 11) and perhaps *nam prik deng* (page 14) are useful to have on hand. They keep for a long time in the refrigerator and freeze indefinitely. Attractively packaged with a sample recipe, they make thoughtful gifts.

If you freeze a batch in an ice cube tray and transfer the cubes to a plastic bag in the freezer, you will find that the preparation of Thai food is vastly simplified. Think of these pastes as extraordinarily powerful bouillon cubes. One cube is all you need to deliver complexity and richness to soups, sauces and stir-fries.

Unlike the dry curries of India, Thai curries are soupy. The liquid is largely composed of coconut milk or cream, both of which are staples in Thai cooking. Making it from scratch, however, is a rather tedious chore that involves cracking open the coconut, prying the meat from the shell, peeling off the brown inner husk and grating the meat. At the end of this process, you are sure to have blistered fingers. Instead, buy the canned product if it is available in your local markets or make it from unsweetened desiccated coconut (recipe on page 112). Once you have made up a batch, freeze it in plastic bags or containers in 1 cup/8 fl oz/250 ml portions.

Except for noodles, which are eaten with chopsticks, Thai food is meant to be eaten with a fork and spoon. Use the fork to transfer a combination of rice and savoury dish to the spoon.

"Serves 4–6" means that the recipe will serve four as a solo main course, and six if you are serving other dishes with it.

Amounts given for ingredients are guidelines only. You may, for example, increase chillies if you prefer the dish hotter, add more prawn paste or fish sauce if you prefer it saltier. You may add or subtract garlic, or leave out certain ingredients altogether. Feel free to modify and experiment. There is no right or wrong. Thai cooking is fluid and forgiving, as well as delicious.

GANG PET
(RED CURRY PASTE)

Makes about 1 cup/8 oz/250 g

2 teaspoons caraway seed
1 teaspoon coriander seed
2$^1/_2$ teaspoons red pepper flakes
3 stalks fresh lemon grass (white part only), snipped into
$^1/_2$ inch/1 cm pieces, or 1$^1/_2$ tablespoons dried
1 inch/2.5 cm piece galangal root, peeled, or 2 tablespoons laos
powder
2 large shallots or 1 medium-size red onion, peeled
8 garlic cloves, peeled
1 tablespoon Prawn Paste (page 15)
1 tablespoon chopped kaffir or regular lime peel
about 3 tablespoons vegetable oil

1. Dry-fry the caraway and coriander seed over low heat for 5 minutes or until fragrant. Grind to a powder.

2. Grind the remaining ingredients in a mini-processor, adding oil as needed to make a smooth, thick paste.

3. Add the caraway and coriander powder and mix thoroughly.

4. Store in an airtight jar in the refrigerator.

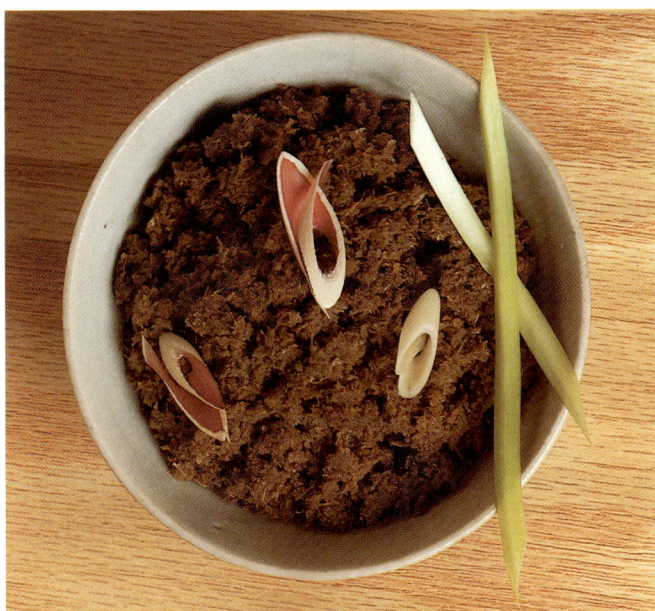

KEO WAN
(GREEN CURRY PASTE)

Makes about 1 cup/8 oz/250 g

3 pieces dried kaffir lime peel
2 teaspoons coriander seed
2 teaspoons black peppercorns
1 inch/2.5 cm piece fresh galangal root, peeled and sliced
$^{1}/_{4}$ cup/2 fl oz/60 ml warm water
7 serrano chillies, stemmed
2 tablespoons chopped lemon grass, white part only
$^{1}/_{4}$ cup/$^{1}/_{2}$ oz/15 g chopped coriander root
$^{1}/_{2}$ medium-size yellow onion
8 garlic cloves, peeled
1 tablespoon Prawn Paste (page 15)
2 tablespoons vegetable oil

1. In a spice grinder, pulverise the lime peel, coriander seed and peppercorns to a powder.

2. Combine the ground spices, galangal, water, chillies, lemon grass, coriander root, onion, garlic and prawn paste in a mini-processor and grind to a paste. Add the oil and pulse the processor once or twice to mix it well.

3. Transfer the paste to an airtight container. It will keep for at least a month in the refrigerator and can be frozen indefinitely.

GANG LUANG
(ORANGE CURRY PASTE)

Makes about 1 cup/8 oz/250 g

This is a general all-purpose paste for curries, vegetables, soups, pork, beef and chicken.

$^1/_2$ cup/2 oz/60 g red chillies, stemmed
1 medium-size red onion, cut into chunks
1 head garlic, peeled
grated peel of 1 lime or lemon
2 tablespoons Prawn Paste (page 15)
1 teaspoon salt

Combine all ingredients in a mini-processor and grind to a paste. The paste will keep for weeks in the refrigerator or indefinitely in the freezer.

NAM PRIK PAO
(ROASTED CURRY PASTE)

Makes about ³/₄ cup/6 oz/175 g

Serve with rice and vegetables or stir a teaspoonful into fish soups. Also delicious on toast.

4 teaspoons vegetable oil
8 dried red chillies, stemmed and seeded
8 garlic cloves, peeled
4 shallots, peeled
2 tablespoons Prawn Paste (page 15)
2 tablespoons dried prawns
2 tablespoons tamarind concentrate
1 tablespoon palm or brown sugar
1 tablespoon fish sauce

1. Heat a wok. Add 1 tablespoon oil and the chillies, garlic and shallots and stir-fry for 2 minutes.

2. Heat the remaining oil and stir-fry the prawn paste about 2 minutes or until its pungent odour has diminished. Transfer to the mini-processor.

3. Add the remaining ingredients to the mini-processor and process to a paste, adding more oil if mixture is too crumbly.

4. Store in an airtight container in the refrigerator for up to 6 months.

GANG PANANG
(PENANG CURRY PASTE)

Makes about $^2/_3$ cup/5 oz/150 g

10 to 15 dried red chillies, seeded and soaked
4 shallots or 1 medium-size red onion
10 garlic cloves, peeled
2 tablespoons chopped fresh lemon grass (white part only) or
2 tablespoons dried flakes, soaked
1 inch/2.5 cm piece fresh galangal root or 1 tablespoon laos powder
1 tablespoon chopped kaffir or regular lime peel
$^1/_4$ cup/$^1/_2$ oz/15 g chopped coriander root
1 teaspoon fresh ground pepper
1 teaspoon ground fennel seed
1 teaspoon ground cumin seed
1 tablespoon Prawn Paste (page 15)
about 3 tablespoons vegetable oil

Combine all ingredients in a mini-processor and grind to a paste, adding vegetable oil as needed to assist in the grinding. The paste will keep for weeks in an airtight jar in the refrigerator, or indefinitely in the freezer.

NAM PRIK ONG
(GROUND PORK AND TOMATO SAUCE)

Makes about 3 cups/24 fl oz/750 g

This sauce is excellent over noodles, cubed tofu or rice, as well as on crackers or as a multi-purpose dip.

2 tablespoons vegetable oil
4 shallots, chopped
8 garlic cloves, chopped
12 oz/375 g ground (minced) pork
2 teaspoons Prawn Paste (page 15)
4 peeled canned tomatoes, drained and pureed
2 teaspoons red chilli flakes

1. Heat 1 tablespoon of the oil in a wok and stir-fry the shallots and garlic until dark golden brown.

2. Heat the remaining tablespoon of oil in the wok. Add the ground pork and stir-fry, breaking up the lumps with a fork, about 2 minutes.

3. Add the prawn paste and stir-fry until the pork loses its pinkness, about 5 minutes.

4. Stir in the pureed tomatoes and chilli flakes and bring to the boil. Lower heat to medium and cook uncovered for 5–10 minutes.

NAM PRIK DENG
(RED CHILLI SAUCE)

Makes about $^2/_3$ cup/5 oz/150 g

Good with raw or cooked vegetables and over rice. Add a spoonful to fish soups and poaching liquids.

8 garlic cloves, peeled
8 red chillies, stemmed
4 large shallots or 1 medium-size red onion, peeled and halved
3 tablespoons Prawn Paste (page 15)
1 small dried salted fish or 1 can sardines, drained
1 tablespoon vegetable oil
2 tablespoons fish sauce
2 teaspoons sugar
juice of $^1/_2$ lime

1. In a hot wok or frying pan, dry-fry garlic, chillies and shallots until slightly charred, about 5 minutes.

2. Transfer the garlic, chillies and shallots to a food processor. Add the prawn paste and fish and grind to a paste.

3. Heat the oil and stir-fry the paste over medium heat for about 5 minutes.

4. Add the fish sauce, sugar and lime juice and mix thoroughly. *Nam prik deng* will keep for months in an airtight container in the refrigerator.

KAPI
(PRAWN PASTE)

Makes about 1 cup/8 oz/250 g

2 lb/1 kg smallest raw prawns, in shells
1 cup/8 oz/250 g rock salt

1. Wash and drain the prawns, leaving the shells on.

2. Mix the prawns with the salt. Cover and refrigerate for 12–24 hours.

3. Grind the prawns and shells to a fine paste in a food processor. Form the paste into 5 patties about 2 inches/5 cm thick. Let dry on a plate on a sunny windowsill for a day, turning every now and then. Repeat this process twice more, breaking up the patties and reforming and reshaping the prawn paste into patties of the same dimensions.

4. After the third time, place paste in an airtight container and let ripen for 2–3 months. Because of its high salt content, the paste will keep indefinitely without refrigeration.

NAM PRIK KAPI
(PRAWN PASTE SAUCE)

Makes about $^1/_2$ cup/4 fl oz/125 ml

Serve as a dipping sauce for steamed chicken, fish and vegetables.

2 teaspoons sugar
2 tablespoons fish sauce
1 tablespoon tamarind water or juice of 1 lime
5 garlic cloves, finely chopped
2 serrano chillies, stemmed and finely chopped
2 teaspoons Prawn Paste (page 15)

1. Dissolve the sugar in the fish sauce.

2. Combine with the tamarind water, garlic, chillies and prawn paste. Transfer to a sauce bowl.

SAUS PRIK
(CHILLI GARLIC SAUCE)

Makes about 2 cups/16 fl oz/500 ml

Good with cold or hot roasted, grilled or barbecued meats, stir-fries, fried chicken, prawns, noodles, fried vegetables, etc. The longer you keep it, the better the flavour. Like most Thai recipes, this is flexible; a variety of flavours can be achieved by mixing and matching ingredients.

$^{1}/_{2}$ cup/4 oz/125 g firmly packed palm or brown sugar
1 cup/8 fl oz/250 ml rice vinegar or cider vinegar
$^{1}/_{3}$ cup/2 oz/60 g currants or seedless raisins, or
1 very ripe peeled banana
2 heads garlic, peeled (about 26 cloves)
2 tablespoons red chilli flakes
1 tablespoon salt

1. Grind all ingredients to a paste in a food processor. Transfer to a stainless steel saucepan.

2. Bring to the boil and cook until mixture becomes syrupy, stirring constantly. The sauce keeps for months in an airtight jar in the refrigerator.

PRIK DONG NAM SOM
(CHILLIES IN VINEGAR)

Makes about 1 cup/8 oz/250 g

This condiment may be found in glass jars on most Thai tables.

$^3/_4$ cup/6 fl oz/175 ml rice vinegar or cider vinegar
1 tablespoon fish sauce
$^1/_2$ cup/2 oz/60 g tiny red and green bird chillies, stemmed (or
substitute thinly sliced serrano chillies)

Combine all ingredients. Let cure 1–2 weeks if using whole chillies; sliced chillies may be used immediately. The chillies will keep about a month refrigerated.

PRIK MANAO
(CHILLI-LIME SAUCE)

Makes about $^1/_2$ cup/4 fl oz/125 ml

This is a wonderful dipping sauce for roasted or barbecued meats and fish. It does not keep; make it fresh each time you use it.

6 red chillies, stemmed and finely sliced
4 garlic cloves, finely chopped
$^1/_2$ cup/4 fl oz/125 ml fresh lime juice
3 tablespoons fish sauce

Combine all ingredients in a dipping bowl and serve the same day.

SAUS SRIRACHA
(SRIRACHA SAUCE)

Makes about 1 cup/8 fl oz/250 ml

This sauce is available in plastic squeeze bottles in most Asian markets. In Southeast Asia, it is used as a table condiment much as Westerners use tomato sauce. Beware: it's fiery!

1 cup/5 oz/150 g dried red chillies, stemmed and soaked in warm water
$^1/_2$ cup/2 oz/60 g garlic cloves, peeled
1 tablespoon sugar
2 teaspoons salt
$^1/_2$ cup/4 fl oz/125 ml vinegar

1. Drain the chillies, reserving the soaking liquid.

2. Process the chillies with the remaining ingredients to a puree, adding soaking liquid if needed to make the sauce a thin consistency.

3. Store in an airtight jar in the refrigerator.

MAH HOA
(PINEAPPLE SLICES TOPPED WITH SPICY PORK)

Makes about 40 pieces

$^1/_2$ cup/4 oz/120 g chopped roasted peanuts
1 tablespoon prawn powder
1–2 tablespoons fish sauce depending on saltiness desired
1 inch/2.5 cm piece fresh ginger, peeled and finely chopped
2 teaspoons sugar (if pineapple is ripe, use only 1 teaspoon)
1 tablespoon tamarind juice or lime juice
1 tablespoon minced coriander root (optional)
$^1/_2$ teaspoon red chilli flakes
8 oz/250 g ground (minced) pork
2 teaspoons cornflour
$^1/_4$ cup/2 fl oz/60 ml cold water
1 unripe pineapple
2 tablespoons Crisp-fried Onion Garnish (page 99)
2 tablespoons Crisp-fried Garlic or Shallot Garnish (page 98)
Garnish:
coriander sprigs

1. Combine the peanuts, prawn powder, fish sauce, ginger, sugar, tamarind juice, coriander root and chilli flakes in a bowl.

2. In a frying pan, dry-fry the pork until cooked through. Drain off fat. Scrape the pork into the bowl with the peanut mixture.

3. Mix the cornflour with the cold water and stir into the pork mixture. Return the mixture to the frying pan and simmer for 3 minutes or until thickened. Remove from heat.

4. Quarter the pineapple lengthwise and remove the skin. Cut each quarter crosswise into triangular slices about $^1/_4$ inch/5 mm thick. Arrange slices on a serving platter.

5. Mound a spoonful of pork mixture onto each triangle, pressing down with the back of a fork.

6. Sprinkle with fried onion and fried garlic.

7. Garnish with coriander sprigs. Serve warm.

KANAM PUNG NA MU
(SPICED PORK AND PRAWN TOAST)

Makes 40 pieces

$^1/_2$ cup/4 oz/125 g ground pork
$^1/_2$ cup/4 oz/125 g prawns, shelled and deveined
1 tablespoon finely chopped coriander roots and leaves
2 spring (green) onions, chopped
2 garlic cloves, finely chopped
1 teaspoon black pepper
1 tablespoon fish sauce
1 egg
10 slices stale bread, crusts removed, quartered
$^1/_2$ cup/4 fl oz/125 ml vegetable oil
Chilli-garlic Sauce (page 17) or Sriracha Sauce (page 20)

1. Combine the pork, prawns, coriander, spring onions, garlic, pepper, fish sauce and egg and beat vigorously.

2. Spread 1 tablespoon meat mixture on each bread square.

3. Heat oil in a wok or frying pan. Cook 5 or 6 bread squares at a time in the hot oil, meat side up, turning once with a slotted spatula so that both sides turn golden and the meat is no longer pink. Drain on paper towels. Repeat until all the squares are cooked. Serve hot with chilli-garlic sauce or Sriracha sauce.

MU WARN
(SWEET PORK)

Serves 4–6

Thinly sliced liver may be substituted for pork. This dish may be served as a main course or an appetiser.

1 lb/500 g lean pork (loin or centre cut), cut into pieces about
2 x 1 x ¼ inch/5 cm x 2.5 cm x 5 mm
1 tablespoon cornflour
2 tablespoons palm or brown sugar
2 teaspoons black pepper
2–3 tablespoons fish sauce
10 garlic cloves, peeled
5 or 6 sprigs coriander with roots
3 tablespoons vegetable oil
½ cup/4 fl oz/125 ml water
1 cup/2 oz/60 g Crisp-fried Onion Garnish (page 99)
or Crisp-fried Shallot Garnish (page 98)

1. Place the pork in a bowl and mix with the cornflour.

2. Combine the sugar, pepper, fish sauce, garlic and coriander in a mini-processor and grind to a paste.

3. Heat the oil in a wok or frying pan and fry the paste for a few seconds.

4. Add the pork and stir-fry over high heat for 3–4 minutes.

5. Stir in the water and reduce heat to low. Cover and simmer for 20 minutes, or until most of the liquid has evaporated and the meat is coated with a thick gravy.

6. Toss the meat with fried onions and serve.

MU SAP TORDIKROB
(SPICY PORK PATTIES)

Makes about 20

1 lb/500 g ground (minced) pork
8 garlic cloves, finely chopped
3 tablespoons fish sauce
1 tablespoon soy sauce
2 serrano chillies, stemmed and minced
2 teaspoons black pepper
2 teaspoons ground coriander
1 teaspoon sugar
$^{1}/_{4}$ cup/2 fl oz/60 ml vegetable oil
Sriracha Sauce (page 20) or Chilli-lime Sauce (page 19)

1. Combine the pork, garlic, fish sauce, soy sauce, chillies, pepper, coriander and sugar and mix well.

2. Form 1 tablespoon of the pork mixture into a ball, then flatten into a patty. Repeat with the remaining mixture.

3. Place the patties on a plate 1 inch/2.5 cm smaller than your steamer rack and set in a wok. Bring water to a boil in the bottom of the wok, cover and steam the patties for 10 minutes.

4. Dry the wok thoroughly. Heat the oil. Fry the patties 5 or 6 at a time until golden. Drain. Serve with Sriracha sauce or chilli-lime sauce.

TORD MUN PLA
(FRIED FISH CAKES WITH GREEN BEANS AND CORIANDER)

Makes 15–20 patties

1 lb/500 g firm white fish fillets, chopped, or 1 lb/500 g commercially prepared fish paste*
$1/4$ teaspoon salt dissolved in 2 tablespoons water (omit if using fish paste)
1–2 tablespoons fish sauce
$1/2$ teaspoon sugar
1 teaspoon red chilli flakes
5 oz/150 g green beans, finely chopped
1 tablespoon minced coriander roots
2 tablespoons cornflour
1 cup/8 fl oz/250 ml vegetable oil
Cucumber Condiment with Chilli (page 103)

1. Purée the fish and the salt water to a smooth paste in a food processor.

2. In a bowl, combine the fish sauce, sugar, chilli flakes, beans and coriander root.

3. Scrape the fish paste into the bowl and sprinkle with the cornflour. Beat vigorously until the mixture is smooth and glistening.

4. Heat the oil to medium-high and drop the fish mixture by tablespoonfuls into the oil, flattening each spoonful into a patty about 2 inches/5 cm in diameter and $1/2$ inch/1 cm thick. Fry the patties until golden brown, adding oil if necessary. Drain on paper towels. Serve hot with chilled cucumber condiment.

*Available in Chinese markets.

PRIK YAT SAI
(PORK-STUFFED GREEN CHILLIES WITH EGG NETS)

Serves 6

8 oz/250 g prawns, shelled and deveined
8 oz/250 g ground (minced) pork
8 sprigs coriander, with roots
6 garlic cloves, peeled
1 inch/2.5 cm piece fresh ginger, peeled and coarsely chopped
2 serrano chillies, stemmed
$1/2$ teaspoon black pepper
2 tablespoons fish sauce
6 long (about 6 inches/15 cm) mild green chillies, seeded and halved
lengthwise or seeded, stemmed and left whole
1 tablespoon vegetable oil, plus 1 teaspoon for brushing the chillies
1 egg, lightly beaten
Chilli-garlic Sauce (page 17)

1. Grind the prawns, pork, coriander, garlic, ginger, serrano chillies, pepper and fish sauce to a paste in a food processor.* Transfer to a bowl.

2. Stuff the pork/prawn mixture into the chilli shells. Place the chillies on a plate at least 1 inch/2.5 cm smaller than the diameter of the steamer to allow the steam to circulate. Set the plate on the steamer rack and bring the water to the boil beneath it. Cover and steam the stuffed chillies for 15 minutes.

3. Meanwhile, heat the oil in a wok over medium heat. Hold a pair of chopsticks in one hand and dip it into the beaten egg mixture. Trail the egg across the wok in one direction. Dip the chopsticks into the egg again and trail the egg in the other direction, crisscrossing to form a net. When golden brown and set (about 2 minutes), remove from the pan. Continue the process until all the egg is used up.

4. To serve, transfer the stuffed chillies to a serving plate and brush with oil to make them shiny. Cover each stuffed chilli with an egg net. Serve hot or at room temperature with chilli garlic sauce.

*This basic pork/prawn paste may be made into patties and fried or steamed, or steamed and then fried. To make patties, wet hands first so the mixture will not stick.

GUNG SONG KEUNG
(CORN AND PRAWN CAKES)

Serves 6

6 garlic cloves
5 sprigs coriander
$1/4$ teaspoon red chilli flakes
$1/4$ teaspoon sugar
2 tablespoons fish sauce
2 cups/8 oz/250 g fresh or frozen sweetcorn
5 oz/150 g prawns, shelled, deveined and coarsely chopped
2 tablespoons cornflour
2 eggs, lightly beaten
$1/2$ cup/4 fl oz/125 ml vegetable oil
Sriracha Sauce (page 20)

1. Grind the garlic, coriander, chilli flakes, sugar and fish sauce to a paste in a food processor. Scrape into a mixing bowl.

2. Place the corn kernels in the processor and pulse once to chop coarsely. Add to the seasoning paste.

3. Add the prawns to the bowl. Sprinkle the mixture with cornflour and stir through.

4. Add the eggs to the bowl and mix well.

5. Heat the oil in a wok. Drop the corn mixture by rounded tablespoonfuls into the hot oil and fry until brown, turning once. Drain on paper towels. Serve hot with Sriracha sauce.

MAMEUNG NAM PRIK PLA WAN
(GREEN MANGOES WITH CHILLI PRAWN SAUCE)

Serves 4

This is a simple appetiser. Any tart green apple may be substituted for the mango. The combination of the sour fruit dipped in the salty fish sauce is unusual and quite addictive.

$^{1}/_{2}$ cup/4 oz/125 g sugar
$^{1}/_{4}$ cup/2 fl oz/60 ml fish sauce
2 fresh red chillies, thinly sliced, or $^{1}/_{2}$ teaspoon red chilli flakes
1 tablespoon prawn powder
2 green mangoes (or green apples), cut into fingers like French fries
and kept in acidulated water (water with lemon juice or vinegar) until
ready to serve

1. In a glass or stainless steel saucepan, cook the sugar with the fish sauce over low heat for 3–5 minutes or until the mixture bubbles and the sugar dissolves.

2. Stir in the chillies and prawn powder.

3. Place the sauce in a bowl in the centre of a platter. Surround with the drained mango or apple fingers and serve.

SATÉ

(BEEF, PORK OR CHICKEN SATAY WITH PEANUT SAUCE)

Serves 4–6

Marinade:
1$^1/_2$ teaspoons vegetable oil
10 garlic cloves, chopped
1$^1/_2$ cups/12 fl oz/375 ml coconut cream
1 tablespoon fish sauce
1 teaspoon turmeric
1 teaspoon Red, Orange or Roasted Curry Paste (optional) (pages 8 to 11)
1$^1/_2$ lb/750 g sirloin steak, pork loin or chicken breasts
Peanut Sauce:
$^1/_2$ cup/4 oz/125 g peanut butter
4 garlic cloves, peeled
1 shallot or $^1/_4$ red onion, peeled
1 teaspoon red chilli flakes
$^1/_4$ cup/2 fl oz/60 ml chicken stock

1. Heat the oil in a saucepan. Add the garlic and sauté over medium heat until golden. Pour in the coconut cream and stir until blended. Set aside one-third of the sauce for dipping.

2. Mix the fish sauce, turmeric and curry paste with the remaining sauce. Set aside.

3. Cut the meat across the grain into 1$^1/_2$ x $^1/_4$ inch/3.5 x 5 cm strips. Place the meat in the marinade and toss to coat thoroughly. Cover and refrigerate overnight.

4. Thread meat on skewers. Grill over hot coals or under a preheated griller. Serve with the remaining garlic-coconut cream and peanut sauce.

For the peanut sauce, combine peanut butter, garlic, shallot, red chilli flakes and chicken stock in a blender or food processor and puree. Transfer to a small saucepan and warm gently over low heat. Serve warm.

KAPI LON
(SPICY PRAWN DIP)

Serves 4–6

1$^1/_2$ cups/12 fl oz/375 ml water
1 lb/500 g small to medium prawns, in shells
8 red chillies, stemmed
8 garlic cloves, peeled
3 large shallots or $^1/_2$ medium-size red onion, peeled
2 tablespoons fish sauce
juice of $^1/_2$ lime
Suggested Vegetables for Dipping:
daikon (white radish)
carrot
Chinese cabbage
celery
Brussels sprouts

1. Bring the water to the boil in a small saucepan. Add prawns and let water return to the boil.

2. Remove prawns, reserving stock. Peel prawns and discard shells.

3. In a wok over high heat, dry-fry the chillies, garlic and shallots until softened and slightly charred, about 5 minutes.

4. Combine the chilli mixture with the prawns and grind to a paste in a food processor. Transfer to a mixing bowl.

5. Stir in the fish sauce, $^1/_4$ cup/2 fl oz/60 ml of the strained prawn stock and the lime juice and mix well.

6. Transfer to a dip bowl and surround with vegetables.

GAENG DOM MU GAI
(CHICKEN SOUP WITH PORK AND EGG STRIPS)

Serves 6–8

2 tablespoons vegetable oil
4 eggs, beaten
1 lb/500 g lean boneless pork, cut into 1 x $^1/_8$ inch/2.5 cm x 3 mm
slices
6 garlic cloves, minced
$^1/_8$ teaspoon black pepper
2 qt/2 l chicken stock
2 teaspoons sugar
1 tablespoon vinegar
1 tablespoon soy sauce
6 spring (green) onions, minced
2 jalapeño or serrano chillies, thinly sliced

1. Heat half the oil in a frying pan. Pour in the beaten egg and tilt the pan to make one large, thin omelette. Let cool. Cut into 2 x $^1/_2$ inch/5 x 1 cm strips and set aside.

2. Mix the pork with the garlic and pepper.

3. Heat the remaining tablespoon of oil and brown the pork on all sides. Set aside.

4. Combine the stock, sugar, vinegar and soy sauce in a 4–5 quart/5 l saucepan and bring to the boil. Remove from heat. Ladle into a serving bowl.

5. Add the egg strips, pork, spring onions and chillies. Serve hot.

EN TOON PAKARD HOM
(TENDER BEEF AND ROMAINE (COS) SOUP WITH MEATBALLS)

Serves 8–10

1 lb/500 g (about 2) beef tendons, rinsed in cold water
5 qt/5 l water or beef stock
2 teaspoons salt
Meatballs:
1$^1/_2$ lb/750 g lean ground (minced) beef
8 garlic cloves, pressed
6 spring (green) onions, minced
10 sprigs coriander with roots, minced
1 teaspoon black pepper
1 tablespoon fish sauce
2 heads romaine (cos) lettuce, cut crosswise into 1 inch/2.5 cm strips
1 packed cup/2 oz/60 g celery leaves

1. Combine the tendons, stock and salt in a large saucepan and cook 3–4 hours or until the tendons are tender. Skim the fat. Cut the tendons crosswise into $^3/_4$ inch/2 cm slices, then into $^3/_4$ inch/2 cm dice.

2. Combine the beef, garlic, spring onions, coriander, pepper and fish sauce. Form into 1 inch/2.5 cm balls. Drop into the stock and simmer 7–10 minutes. Skim fat. Remove from heat.

3. Place the romaine and celery leaves in the bottom of a large serving bowl. Pour the soup over the greens and serve at once.

EN TOON
(TENDER BEEF SOUP)

Serves 10–12

3 beef tendons (about 1½ lb/750 g), rinsed in cold water
5 qt/5 l water
3 inch/7.5 cm cinnamon sticks
3 star anise
2 inch/5 cm piece of galangal or 2 teaspoons laos powder
¼ cup/2 fl oz/60 ml soy sauce
½ cup/4 fl oz/125 ml fish sauce
1 tablespoon sugar
Garnish:
8 oz/250 g bean sprouts
coriander sprigs
5 spring (green) onions, sliced diagonally into 1 inch/2.5 cm pieces
Crisp-fried Garlic (page 98), optional

1. Combine the beef, water, cinnamon, anise, galangal and soy sauce in a large saucepan and bring to the boil. Reduce heat and simmer for 3 hours. Remove from heat and lift beef from stock.

2. When it is cool enough to handle, slice the beef crosswise into ¾ inch/2 cm pieces, then dice into ¾ inch/2 cm pieces. Return to the stock and cook for another hour or until completely tender.

3. Add the fish sauce and sugar, stirring well to dissolve the sugar.

4. Place the bean sprouts in a large serving bowl and ladle the soup on top. Garnish with the remaining ingredients.

DOM YOM GAI NAM PRIK DENG
(CHICKEN SOUP WITH RED CHILLI SAUCE)

Serves 8–10

2–3 lb/1–1.5 kg chicken or 3 lb/1.5 kg chicken parts
1 teaspoon Red Chilli Sauce (page 14)
1 tablespoon minced garlic
1 tablespoon minced coriander root
3 spring (green) onions
2 serrano chillies, stemmed and thinly sliced
juice of $\frac{1}{2}$ lime
2 tablespoons fish sauce
2 teaspoons laos powder
1 teaspoon prawn powder
Garnish:
1 tablespoon minced garlic
1 tablespoon minced fresh ginger
6 spring (green) onions, chopped
1 tablespoon minced coriander leaves
2 tablespoons soy sauce
2 tablespoons fish sauce
8 oz/250 g cooked tiny prawns

1. Combine the first 10 ingredients in a large saucepan and add enough water to cover the chicken. Bring to the boil, then turn off heat. Cover the saucepan and let stand 45 minutes or until the chicken is cooked through.

2. Meanwhile, assemble the garnish ingredients in a deep serving bowl.

3. When the chicken is opaque and the juices run clear, remove it from the pan.

4. When it is cool enough to handle, remove the meat from the bones and shred the meat. Discard the bones and skin.

5. Place the shredded chicken on top of the garnishes.

6. Ladle in the stock and serve at once.

DOM YOM GUNG
(SOUR PRAWN SOUP)

Serves 6–8

2 qt/2 l water
4 stalks lemon grass
1 lb/500 g medium prawns, peeled and deveined
1 cup/4 oz/125 g tinned straw mushrooms
2 kaffir lime leaves
$^1/_2$ cup/4 fl oz/125 ml fish sauce
1 tablespoon Roasted Curry Paste (page 11)
$^1/_2$ cup/2 oz/60 g minced coriander root
juice of 2 limes
8 serrano chillies, thinly sliced
steamed rice

1. Boil the water with the lemon grass in a large saucepan for 10 minutes, covered.

2. Add the prawns, mushrooms, lime leaves, fish sauce, curry paste and coriander root and return to the boil. Cook until prawns turn pink, about 3–4 minutes.

3. Remove from heat. Discard lemon grass and stir in the lime juice and chillies. Serve at once with rice.

GANG JUD TOHU
(STUFFED BEANCAKE SOUP)

Serves 6–8

$^{1}/_{2}$ cup/2 oz/60 g coriander roots
6 garlic cloves, peeled
1 tablespoon fish sauce
$^{1}/_{4}$ teaspoon black pepper
1 lb/500 g ground (minced) pork
2 tablespoons cornflour
2 x 1 lb/500 g packages firm tofu
2 qt/2 l chicken stock
$^{1}/_{4}$ cup/2 fl oz/60 ml fish sauce
12 oz/375 g medium prawns, peeled, deveined and halved
lengthwise
Garnish:
6 spring (green) onions, cut diagonally into 1 inch/2.5 cm pieces
coriander sprigs
4 serrano chillies, thinly sliced
steamed rice

1. Grind coriander roots, garlic, fish sauce and pepper to a paste in a mini-processor.

2. Mix well with the pork and cornflour.

3. Drain the tofu and pat dry. Cut each slice into quarters. Cut a pocket into each piece with a knife. Stuff each pocket with 1 teaspoon pork mixture and gently press down on top. Place the pieces on a plate 1 inch/2.5 cm smaller in diameter than the steamer.

4. Bring water to the boil in the bottom of the steamer. Set the plate on the steamer rack and steam the tofu envelopes for 5–7 minutes.

5. Bring the stock to the boil. Reduce heat and add the fish sauce, prawns and tofu pieces. Simmer for 5 minutes. Transfer to a serving bowl.

6. Garnish with spring onions, coriander and serrano chillies. Serve with steamed rice.

KAI KEM YUM
(SALTED EGG SALAD)

Serves 6

6 Salted Eggs (page 100), hard-boiled and shelled
6 leaves butter (leaf) lettuce
1 large red onion, thinly sliced
6 spring (green) onions, cut diagonally into $^3/_4$ inch/2 cm pieces
1 large carrot, julienned
3 red and/or green serrano chillies, stemmed and slivered
coriander sprigs
2 limes, cut into wedges
Dressing:
2 tablespoons fish sauce
1 tablespoon palm or brown sugar
juice of $^1/_2$ lime
$^1/_4$ teaspoon red chilli flakes

1. Thinly slice the eggs. Arrange the lettuce on a platter. Add the onion, then the egg slices, then the spring onions. Strew the mounded salad with the carrot, chilli strips and coriander sprigs. Surround with lime wedges.

2. For the dressing, combine the fish sauce, sugar, lime juice and chilli flakes. Spoon over the salad and serve.

LARB NUA
(SPICY GROUND MEAT WITH MINT LEAVES)

Serves 6–8

1½ lb/750 g ground (minced) beef, chicken, pork or turkey
4 garlic cloves, finely chopped
⅓ cup/2½ fl oz/80 ml fish sauce
⅓ cup/2½ fl oz/80 ml lime juice
½ teaspoon red chilli flakes
6–8 leaves butter (leaf) or romaine (cos) lettuce
2 tablespoons toasted pulverised rice*
1 large red onion, thinly sliced
15 mint leaves

1. Dry-fry the ground meat until cooked through, breaking up clumps with the back of a spoon. Transfer to a bowl and let cool.

2. Combine the garlic, fish sauce, lime juice and red chilli flakes. Pour over the meat and mix through.

3. Arrange the lettuce leaves on a serving platter. Divide the meat mixture into even portions and spoon into the lettuce leaves.

4. Sprinkle on the rice powder, then strew with onion slices and mint leaves. Serve at room temperature.

*For toasted rice: Heat a wok and dry-fry 1 cup/7 oz/200 g raw rice until golden, stirring and tossing so that the kernels colour evenly. Grind to a coarse powder in a spice grinder. Keep on hand in a covered airtight jar.

SOM TAM
(GREEN PAPAYA SALAD)

Serves 4–6

2 green papayas, peeled, seeded and shredded
4 carrots, peeled and shredded
$^3/_4$ cup/3 oz/90 g green beans, julienned and cut into 2 inch/5 cm
lengths
1 tablespoon palm or brown sugar
juice of 2 limes
1 tablespoon fish sauce
3 garlic cloves, finely chopped
$^1/_3$ cup/1 oz/30 g prawn powder
4–6 leaves butter (leaf) or iceberg lettuce
$^1/_3$ cup/2 oz/60 g chopped roasted peanuts
coriander sprigs

1. Combine the papayas, carrots and beans in a mixing bowl.

2. Combine the sugar, lime juice and fish sauce, stirring until the sugar is dissolved. Stir in the garlic and prawn powder. Pour the dressing over the papaya mixture and toss thoroughly.

3. Arrange the lettuce leaves on a serving platter and mound the papaya mixture in the centre.

4. Sprinkle with peanuts, strew with coriander sprigs and serve.

YUM GUNG TOUKAG
(PRAWN AND GREEN BEAN SALAD)

Serves 6

12 oz/375 g medium prawns, shelled and deveined
12 oz/375 g slender green beans or Chinese long beans, cut
diagonally into 2 inch/5 cm pieces
2 garlic cloves, finely chopped
1 teaspoon prawn powder
1 teaspoon Prawn Paste (page 15)
$\frac{1}{2}$ teaspoon red chilli flakes
1 teaspoon sugar
2 tablespoons tamarind water (page 115), or lemon or lime juice
2 tablespoons fish sauce

1. Cook the prawns in boiling water just until opaque and pink, about 2 minutes. Plunge into cold water and drain. When cool enough to handle, cut each prawn in half lengthwise. Transfer to a mixing bowl.

2. Blanch the beans 1 minute, then plunge into cold water and drain. Add to the prawns.

3. Combine the garlic, prawn powder, prawn paste, chilli flakes, sugar, tamarind water and fish sauce and stir until the sugar is dissolved. Pour the dressing over the prawns and green beans and mix thoroughly.

4. Chill and serve.

SOMOR YUM JAI
(POMELO CHICKEN SALAD)

Serves 6

Available in Asian markets, pomelos are similar to grapefruits but have thicker skins and fewer membranes. Grapefruits may be substituted.

$1/2$ teaspoon red chilli flakes
1 tablespoon fish sauce
1 teaspoon sugar
juice of 2 limes
6 leaves iceberg or butter (leaf) lettuce
3 pomelos or pink grapefruits, sectioned, membranes removed
4 cooked chicken breasts, skinned, boned and shredded
$1/2$ cup/3 oz/90 g roasted chopped peanuts
Garnish:
$1/2$ cup/3 oz/85 g Crisp-fried Onion Garnish (page 99) or Crisp-fried
Shallot Garnish (page 98)
coriander sprigs
4 red chilli flowers (page 113) or slivered red chillies

1. Combine the chilli flakes, fish sauce, sugar and lime juice, stirring until the sugar dissolves. Set aside.

2. Arrange the lettuce leaves on a round or oval serving plate.

3. Make a ring of pomelo or grapefruit sections in the centre.

4. Fill the ring with the shredded chicken.

5. Pour on the dressing. Garnish with crisp-fried onions, coriander sprigs and chilli flowers. Serve immediately.

YUM GUNG MAMUANG
(PRAWN, GRAPEFRUIT AND GREEN MANGO SALAD)

Serves 6

4 grapefruit
2 cups/16 fl oz/500 ml water
1 tablespoon salt
12 oz/375 g medium prawns, peeled and halved lengthwise
$^1/_4$ cup/2 fl oz/60 ml fish sauce
$1^1/_2$ teaspoons sugar
5 garlic cloves, finely chopped
4 red chillies, thinly sliced
6 lettuce leaves
3 carrots, peeled and shredded
1 green mango or papaya, shredded
Garnish:
coriander sprigs
red chilli flowers (page 113)

1. Peel and section the grapefruit. Holding them over a bowl to catch the juice, remove the membranes.

2. Combine the water and salt in a saucepan and bring to the boil. Drop in the prawns and cook 2 minutes. Plunge into cold water and drain. Set aside.

3. Combine the fish sauce, sugar, garlic, chillies and reserved grapefruit juice, stirring until the sugar is dissolved. Set aside.

4. Line a platter with the lettuce leaves. Make an outer ring of shredded carrots on the lettuce. Inside that, make a ring of shredded mango. Mound the grapefruit sections in the centre of the ring.

5. Arrange the prawns over the top. Cover with plastic wrap and chill.

6. When ready to serve, spoon on the dressing. Garnish with coriander sprigs and red chilli flowers.

YAM YAI
(THE GREAT THAI SALAD)

Serves 6

12 leaves butter (leaf) or iceberg lettuce
$^1/_2$ cup/2 oz/60 g bean sprouts, blanched
1 cucumber, peeled, seeded and julienned
12 cooked prawns, peeled, deveined and halved lengthwise
12 oz/375 g cooked boneless pork, julienned
1 poached chicken breast, skinned, boned and slivered
3 hard-boiled eggs, shelled and quartered
6 cherry tomatoes, halved
Dressing:
3 tablespoons rice vinegar, or white vinegar
2 teaspoons fish sauce
juice of $^1/_2$ lime
2 teaspoons sugar
3 garlic cloves, minced
2 serrano chillies, stemmed and thinly sliced
Garnish:
10 mint or basil leaves

1. Arrange the lettuce leaves on a serving plate.

2. Mound the bean sprouts and cucumber in the centre of the plate. Arrange the prawns, pork and chicken around the perimeter.

3. Decorate the plate with the eggs and cherry tomatoes. Chill.

4. Combine the dressing ingredients, stirring until the sugar is dissolved.

5. When ready to serve, pour the dressing over the salad. Garnish with mint.

YUM MA KUA
(AUBERGINE SALAD)

Serves 6

6 Japanese or Thai aubergines, halved lengthwise
Dressing:
$1/2$ teaspoon palm or brown sugar
1 tablespoon fish sauce
1 tablespoon soy sauce
juice of $1/2$ lime
4 garlic cloves, finely chopped
$1/4$ teaspoon red chilli flakes
1 teaspoon prawn powder
2 tablespoons sesame oil
Garnish:
coriander sprigs
4 spring (green) onions, finely chopped

1. Steam the halved aubergines until tender, about 10 minutes. Transfer to a serving platter.

2. Combine all the dressing ingredients in a jar with a tight-fitting lid and shake well. Spoon over the aubergines.

3. Garnish salad with coriander sprigs and spring onion. Serve warm or at room temperature.

YUM NUR
(BEEF AND ROMAINE (COS) SALAD)

Serves 6

6 romaine (cos) lettuce leaves
1 large cucumber, peeled and thinly sliced
1 medium-size red onion, thinly sliced
$^1/_2$ cup/2 oz/60 g thinly sliced red radishes
1 bunch spring (green) onions, cut diagonally into 1 inch/2.5 cm lengths
12 mint leaves
12 basil leaves
Dressing:
2 tablespoons fish sauce
$^1/_3$ cup/2$^1/_2$ fl oz/ 80 ml lime juice
1 teaspoon sugar
1 tablespoon chopped garlic
1 teaspoon chopped fresh ginger
$^1/_4$ teaspoon red chilli flakes
2 lb/1 kg sirloin steak, grilled rare

1. Arrange lettuce leaves on a serving platter.

2. Combine the cucumber, onion, radishes, spring onions, mint and basil. Mound on top of the lettuce.

3. Combine the dressing ingredients, stirring to dissolve the sugar. Set aside.

4. Cut the steak diagonally into slices $^1/_4$ inch/5 mm thick, saving the juices. Arrange on top of the salad.

5. Mix accumulated meat juices with the dressing. Spoon over the salad and serve while the steak is warm or at room temperature.

YUM PLA MURK
(SQUID SALAD)

Serves 6

12 squid, cleaned, skinned and cut into 1 inch/2.5 cm rings (reserve
tentacles)
1 cup/2 oz/60 g mint leaves
1 red onion, thinly sliced, the layers separated
2 inch/5 cm piece of fresh ginger, peeled and julienned
juice of 1 lime
4 dried red chillies, stemmed, softened in warm water and drained
1 tablespoon vinegar
1 teaspoon sugar
1 tablespoon fish sauce
$^{1}/_{2}$ cup/1 oz/30 g coriander leaves
Garnish:
coriander sprigs
red chilli flowers (page 113) or slivers

1. Blanch the squid rings and tentacles in a large saucepan of boiling
water for 30 seconds, or until just firm and opaque. Drain well.
Transfer to a mixing bowl.

2. Add the mint, red onion and ginger.

3. Combine the lime juice, chillies, vinegar, sugar, fish sauce and
coriander leaves in a mini-processor and purée. Pour over the squid
mixture and toss.

4. Transfer the salad to a serving plate. Garnish with coriander and
red chillies. Serve at room temperature.

GAI YANG
(THAI BARBECUED CHICKEN)

Serves 4–6

$^1/_2$ cup/1 oz/30 g finely chopped coriander sprigs with roots
8 garlic cloves, finely chopped
2 tablespoons fish sauce
1 tablespoon soy sauce
2 teaspoons five-spice powder or powdered turmeric
1 teaspoon red chilli flakes
1 tablespoon palm or brown sugar
$^1/_2$ teaspoon salt
$^1/_3$ cup/$2^1/_2$ fl oz/80 ml coconut cream
1 frying or grilling chicken, split in half
Sriracha Sauce (page 20)

1. Combine all ingredients except the chicken and Sriracha sauce.

2. Smear the mixture onto the chicken, making sure all sides and the cavity are coated. Cover and refrigerate at least 2 hours or overnight.

3. Arrange the chicken halves on a grill or griller pan. Grill over hot coals or grill under a preheated griller about 6 inches from the flame for about 15 minutes on each side or until the skin is brown and crisp and the juices run clear. Serve with Sriracha sauce.

PANANG KRUANG DONG
(COCONUT CHILLI CHICKEN)

Serves 4

4 garlic cloves, peeled
4 shallots, peeled
1 stalk lemon grass (white part only), finely chopped, or 2 teaspoons lemon grass powder
1 handful coriander leaves, stems and roots
1 teaspoon red chilli flakes
1 teaspoon black pepper
3 slices fresh galangal or 1 teaspoon laos powder
1 teaspoon Prawn Paste (page 15)
2 cups/16 fl oz/500 ml coconut cream
2 teaspoons palm or brown sugar
3 tablespoons fish sauce
1 small chicken, skinned and cut into serving pieces
Garnish:
red chilli flowers (page 113)
coriander sprigs

1. Grind the garlic, shallots, lemon grass, coriander, chilli flakes, black pepper, galangal and prawn paste to a coarse paste in a mini-processor.

2. Place $^1/_2$ cup/8 fl oz/250 ml of the coconut cream in a wok or frying pan and heat to medium. Blend in the garlic paste, palm sugar and fish sauce.

3. Add the remaining coconut cream and bring to the boil.

4. Add the chicken and return the mixture to the boil. Reduce heat and simmer uncovered until the coconut cream reduces and thickens, about 30 minutes. Transfer to a serving dish. Garnish with red chilli flowers and coriander sprigs.

GAI DOON KAPI
(STEAMED CHICKEN WITH PRAWN PASTE SAUCE)

Serves 4–6

4 cups/1 qt/1 l water
3–4 lb/1.5–2 kg chicken
1 recipe Prawn Paste Sauce (page 16)
$^1/_2$ head lettuce, shredded
1 cucumber, thinly sliced
Garnish:
coriander sprigs
spring (green) onions, cut diagonally into 1 inch/2.5 cm pieces
red chilli flowers (page 113)

1. Bring the water to the boil in the bottom of a steamer. Place the chicken on the steamer rack. Cover and steam until the juices run clear, 45 minutes to 1 hour. Meanwhile, prepare the prawn paste sauce.

2. When chicken is cool enough to handle, discard the skin, bones and gristle. Cut the meat into bite-sized pieces.

3. Spread the shredded lettuce evenly on a serving platter. Mound the chicken meat in the centre.

4. Surround with cucumber slices and drizzle with prawn paste sauce.

5. Garnish with coriander sprigs, spring onions and red chilli flowers. Serve warm or at room temperature.

GAI TORD
(SIAMESE FRIED CHICKEN)

Serves 6

8 garlic cloves, peeled
2 shallots, peeled, or $^1/_2$ medium-size red onion, quartered
2 serrano chillies, stemmed
2 teaspoons black pepper
roots of 1 bunch coriander, chopped (about $^1/_2$ cup/2 oz/60 g)
2 tablespoons soy sauce
$^1/_2$ teaspoon salt
1 tablespoon vegetable oil
6 chicken legs, rinsed and patted dry
$^1/_2$ cup/4 fl oz/125 ml vegetable oil
Sriracha Sauce (page 20) or Chilli-lime Sauce (page 19)

1. Combine the garlic, shallots, chillies, pepper, coriander roots, soy sauce, salt and 1 tablespoon oil in a mini-processor and grind to a paste. Smear onto the chicken with a rubber spatula. Cover and refrigerate overnight.

2. Heat the remaining oil in a wok or frying pan. Fry the chicken* in batches until brown, being careful not to overcrowd. Drain on paper towels. Serve with Sriracha sauce or chilli-lime sauce.

*Instead of frying, the chicken may be grilled or roasted at this point.

LUK GIN GAI
(CHICKEN PATTIES)

Makes 8–10

6 cups/$1^{1}/_{2}$ qt/1.5 l water
1 tablespoon salt
1 lb/500 g ground (minced) chicken
6–8 garlic cloves
1 tablespoon coriander leaves
2 tablespoons fish sauce
$^{1}/_{2}$ teaspoon white pepper
salt to taste
Sriracha Sauce (page 20), Chilli-garlic Sauce (page 17) or
Chilli-lime Sauce (page 19)

1. Bring the water to the boil in a saucepan with the salt. Meanwhile, grind all remaining ingredients to a smooth, silken paste in a food processor. Season with salt to taste.

2. Reduce heat to simmer. Drop rounded tablespoons of the chicken mixture into the water and cook until the patties rise to the surface. Drain thoroughly on paper towels.

3. At this point the patties may be fried, brushed with oil and grilled, or served as is. Serve with the preferred sauce.

GAI KING
(STIR-FRIED GINGER CHICKEN)

Serves 6

6 whole boneless chicken breasts
2 tablespoons fish sauce
2 tablespoons soy sauce
1 teaspoon sugar
2 tablespoons vegetable oil
1 red onion, sliced
6 garlic cloves, chopped
2 inch/5 cm piece fresh ginger, peeled and thinly sliced
3 red or green serrano chillies, stemmed and cut lengthwise into fine strips
$^1/_4$ teaspoon red chilli flakes
$^1/_4$ cup/$^1/_2$ oz/15 g coarsely chopped mint or basil leaves
Garnish:
whole mint or basil leaves
red chilli flowers (page 113)
steamed rice

1. Cut the chicken breasts into $1^1/_2$ x 1 x $^1/_2$ inch/3.5 x 2.5 x 1 cm pieces. Set aside.

2. Mix the fish sauce, soy sauce and sugar. Set aside.

3. Heat the oil in a wok. Add the onion and garlic and sauté over medium heat until golden brown.

4. Add the chicken pieces and stir-fry until white and opaque.

5. Add the ginger, chillies, chili flakes and fish sauce mixture and cook about 4 minutes or until chicken is just cooked through. Transfer to a serving plate. Garnish with mint or basil leaves and chilli flowers. Serve with rice.

GAI BING KING KRATIEM
(ROASTED CORNISH HENS WITH GINGER-GARLIC SAUCE)

Serves 4–6

$^1/_2$ cup/4 fl oz/125 ml rice, cider or red wine vinegar*
$^1/_2$ cup/4 fl oz/125 ml soy sauce
1 teaspoon palm or brown sugar
1 teaspoon white pepper
1 teaspoon laos (galangal) powder (optional)
8 garlic cloves, chopped
3 tablespoons chopped fresh ginger
2 teaspoons sesame oil
4 Cornish hens or 1 chicken or 4–6 quail, rinsed and patted dry
1 tablespoon cornflour
$^1/_2$ cup/4 fl oz/125 ml rice wine or chicken stock
additional stock as needed
Garnish:
2 red chillies, thinly sliced
6 spring (green) onions, cut diagonally into 1 inch/2.5 cm pieces

1. In a bowl large enough to hold the poultry, combine the vinegar, soy sauce, sugar, pepper, laos, garlic, ginger and sesame oil. Add the poultry and refrigerate 4 hours to overnight, turning occasionally.

2. Preheat oven to 400°F/200°C/Gas 6.

3. Remove poultry from marinade and drain off excess. Reserve marinade.

4. Place poultry in a roasting dish and roast, uncovered, until crisp and brown (approximately 40 minutes for hens, 1 hour for chicken, and 10–20 minutes for quail).

5. Meanwhile, heat the remaining marinade. Dissolve the cornflour in rice wine, stir into the marinade and bring to the boil, adding more stock if sauce is too thick.

6. Transfer the poultry to a serving dish. Spoon on the sauce. Garnish with chillies and spring onions.

*For a completely different taste, substitute coconut cream for the vinegar. Omit the cornflour and water and boil the marinade until it thickens.

GAI TOONG
(BRAISED SPICY CHICKEN)

Serves 4–6

2–3 lb/1–5 kg frying or grilling chicken, disjointed
¼ cup/2 fl oz/60 ml vegetable oil
6 garlic cloves, peeled
3 shallots, peeled and halved
2 serrano chillies, stemmed
1 stalk lemon grass (white part only), coarsely chopped, or 1 teaspoon
powdered
6 coriander sprigs with roots
2 slices fresh galangal root or 1 teaspoon laos powder
1 teaspoon Prawn Paste (page 15)
1 teaspoon Chinese five-spice powder
½ teaspoon salt
3 tablespoons fish sauce
2 tablespoons tamarind water (page 115)
1 cup/8 fl oz/250 ml chicken stock or water
steamed rice

1. Heat the wok over high heat for 1 minute. Add the oil. When it is barely smoking, brown the chicken parts in batches, being careful not to crowd. Remove and set aside, wiping out the wok.

2. Meanwhile, grind the garlic, shallots, chillies, lemon grass, coriander, galangal, prawn paste, Chinese five-spice powder and salt to a paste in a mini-processor.

3. Fry the paste in the wok over medium heat until fragrant, about 3 minutes.

4. Meanwhile, combine the fish sauce, tamarind water and stock.

5. Add the chicken parts and their juices to the wok and stir to coat with the paste.

6. Add the tamarind stock and bring to the boil. Reduce heat, cover and simmer until the chicken is very tender. Serve with rice.

GAI PAD NAM PRIK PAU
(STIR-FRIED CHICKEN BREAST IN ROASTED CURRY PASTE SAUCE)

Serves 4–6

2 tablespoons vegetable oil
2 rounded tablespoons Roasted Curry Paste (page 11)
4 garlic cloves, chopped
2 shallots, sliced
1 lb/500 g boned and skinned chicken breasts, cut into $1^1/_2$ inch/3.5 cm cubes
1 teaspoon sugar
3 tablespoons fish sauce
$^1/_3$–$^1/_2$ cup/$2^1/_2$–4 fl oz/80–125 ml thin coconut milk, water or stock
20 basil leaves
steamed rice

1. Heat half the oil in a wok, swirling to coat the sides. Stir-fry the curry paste, garlic and shallots over medium heat for 2–3 minutes.

2. Add the chicken and stir-fry briefly, basting to coat each piece.

3. Combine the sugar, fish sauce and coconut milk, and add to the chicken. Bring to a rolling boil, stirring constantly.

4. Add the basil leaves, and toss. Serve at once with rice.

GAI DOM JA
(CHICKEN IN COCONUT MILK)

Serves 6

6 chicken legs and 6 thighs (or one 3 lb/1.5 kg chicken, disjointed)
4 kaffir lime leaves (if using dried leaves, soak in warm water for 15 minutes)
1 tablespoon grated lime peel
6 slices fresh galangal
1 teaspoon salt
$^1/_2$ teaspoon black pepper
2 cups/16 fl oz/500 ml coconut cream
2 serrano chillies, stemmed and crushed
$^1/_2$ cup/1 oz/30 g chopped coriander roots and leaves
3 tablespoons fish sauce
3 tablespoons lime juice
Garnish:
coriander leaves
sliced red chillies

1. Combine the chicken, lime leaves, lime peel, galangal, salt, pepper and coconut cream in a saucepan and bring to the boil. Reduce heat and simmer uncovered about 30 minutes, or until the chicken is done and the sauce has thickened.

2. Stir in the chillies, coriander, fish sauce and lime juice. Ladle into serving bowls. Garnish with coriander leaves and chillies.

BAT YANG
(ROAST DUCK)

Serves 4–6

2 whole ducklings, about 3 lb/1.5 kg each
8 garlic cloves, finely chopped
2 teaspoons red chilli flakes
2 teaspoons five-spice powder
1 tablespoon palm or brown sugar
1 tablespoon honey
juice of 1 lemon
2 tablespoons soy sauce
steamed rice
Chilli-garlic Sauce (page 17)

1. Rinse ducks and pat dry. Remove wing tips and discard or reserve for stock. Preheat oven to 450°F/230°C/Gas 8.

2. Combine the remaining ingredients and rub all over the ducks, including the cavities.

3. Place the ducks on a wire rack and roast for 15 minutes. Reduce heat to 375°F/190°/Gas 5 and roast 30 minutes more. Serve with rice and chilli-garlic sauce.

PLA DOON PET
(STEAMED FISH FILLETS WITH HOT BEAN SAUCE)

Serves 4

Sauce:
2 jalapeño or 4 serrano chillies, seeded and stemmed
1 celery stalk, cut into chunks
2 shallots or $1/2$ small red onion, peeled
1 inch/2.5 cm piece of fresh ginger, peeled and coarsely chopped
3 large garlic cloves, peeled
1 tablespoon vegetable oil
1 rounded tablespoon Chinese hot bean paste
1 teaspoon sugar
1 teaspoon soy sauce
1 teaspoon white or cider vinegar
1 tablespoon fish sauce
1 tablespoon cornflour mixed with $3/4$ cup/6 fl oz/175 ml cold water
2 lb/1 kg fillets of sea bass, sole, halibut or ocean perch
Garnish:
coriander sprigs
thinly sliced spring (green) onions and red chillies

1. Combine the chillies, celery, shallots, ginger and garlic in a mini-food processor and grind to a paste.

2. Heat the oil in a wok or saucepan. Add processed ingredients and stir-fry over medium heat for 3–4 minutes or until slightly browned.

3. Stir in the bean paste and sugar and bring to the boil.

4. Stir in the soy sauce, vinegar and fish sauce.

5. Add the cornflour mixture and cook, stirring constantly, until sauce has thickened. Remove from heat.

6. Place the fillets on a plate. Set the plate on the rack of a steamer and steam 10 minutes per inch/2.5 cm of thickness. (Base your calculations on the thickest part of the fillet.) Drain off any liquid that accumulates.

7. Spoon the sauce over the fillets, garnish and serve immediately.

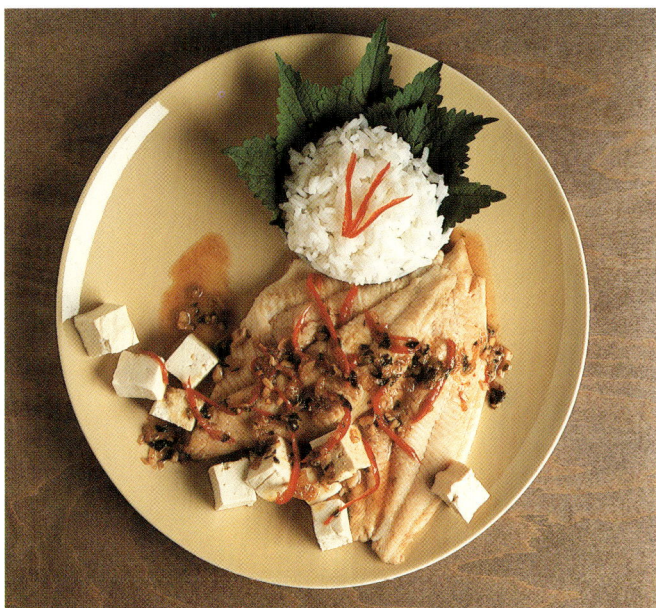

PLA DOM GANG PET TOHU
(CATFISH WITH TOFU CUBES IN CURRY PASTE BROTH)

Serves 4

1 tablespoon vegetable oil
2 serrano chillies, stemmed and thinly sliced
1 large shallot, chopped
4 garlic cloves, chopped
2 teaspoons Red Curry Paste (page 8) or Green Curry Paste (page 9)
2 tablespoons coriander, minced
juice of 1 lime
1 tablespoon fish sauce
$1/2$ teaspoon sugar
1 cup/8 fl oz/250 ml chicken stock
2–3 lb/1–1.5 kg catfish (rock turbot), skinned
1 package (about 1 lb/500 g) firm tofu, drained and cut into
$1/2$ inch/1 cm cubes
steamed rice

1. Heat a wok. Add oil and swirl until the sides are coated.

2. Combine the chillies, shallot, garlic and curry paste. Add to the wok and stir-fry until fragrant, about 10 seconds.

3. Combine the coriander, lime juice, fish sauce, sugar and chicken stock. Add to the wok and bring to the boil.

4. Add the catfish, cover and cook 8 minutes.

5. Add the tofu cubes, cover and cook 2 minutes more.

6. Serve hot with rice. The cooking liquid may be frozen and used for poaching fish and shellfish.

PLA NAM KATEE
(SPICY FISH FILLETS IN COCONUT CREAM)

Serves 4–6

5 garlic cloves, peeled
1 medium-size red onion, peeled and quartered
2 jalapeño chillies, seeded and stemmed, or $^1/_2$ teaspoon red chilli flakes
3 tablespoons fish sauce
$^1/_2$ bunch coriander with roots
1 teaspoon turmeric
$^1/_2$ teaspoon black pepper
1 jumbo or 2 small eggs, beaten
$^3/_4$ cup/6 fl oz/175 ml coconut cream
2 lb/1 kg fillets of sole, red snapper, flounder or other white-fleshed
fish, whole or cut into 1 inch/2.5 cm strips
$^1/_4$ cup/1 oz/30 g rice flour (page 114)
salt
Garnish:
coriander sprigs
red chillies
steamed rice

1. Combine all ingredients except the coconut cream, fish fillets and rice flour in a food processor and liquefy. Transfer to a shallow bowl and mix with the coconut cream.

2. Rinse the fillets and pat dry; salt lightly. Coat each piece with the liquid and drain excess. Place the fillets on a serving plate at least 1 inch/2.5 cm smaller in diameter than the steamer.

3. Dust each fillet with rice flour. (This is more easily accomplished if you put the flour in a shaker.) Wipe the excess from the rim of the plate.

4. Bring the water in the bottom of the steamer to the boil. Place the plate on the steamer rack, cover and steam about 10 minutes.

5. Blot up excess liquid from plate. Garnish with sprigs of coriander and red chillies. Serve immediately with rice.

PLA CHIEN MAKAM
(TAMARIND FISH FILLETS)

Serves 4–6

3 tablespoons vegetable oil
2 lb/1 kg fillets of snapper, sole or other white-fleshed fish
1 large yellow onion, quartered and thinly sliced
2 tablespoons finely chopped garlic
1 tablespoon finely chopped fresh ginger
1 teaspoon tamarind concentrate dissolved in
$^{1}/_{3}$ cup/$2^{1}/_{2}$ fl oz/80 ml warm water
2 tablespoons palm or brown sugar
2 tablespoons fish sauce
3 tablespoons soy sauce
Garnish:
Crisp-fried Onion Garnish (page 99)
thinly sliced spring (green) onions
coriander sprigs

1. Heat the oil in a frying pan until barely smoking. Fry the fish fillets briefly, one at a time, until golden. Transfer to a plate.

2. In the remaining oil, fry the onion and garlic until golden.

3. Add the ginger, tamarind liquid, sugar, fish sauce and soy sauce. Reduce heat and simmer 3 minutes.

4. Return the fillets to the sauce, being careful not to break them. Spoon the sauce over the fish and simmer until it is cooked through, about 2–5 minutes depending on thickness.

5. Carefully transfer the fillets to a serving plate. Spoon the sauce over them. Garnish with the fried onions, spring onions and coriander sprigs. Serve at once.

PU CHA
(CRAB CAKES)

Yields 6 cakes

$^1/_2$ cup/4 fl oz/125 ml vegetable oil
2 shallots or $^1/_2$ medium-size red onion, minced
4 garlic cloves
2 teaspoons Red Curry Paste (page 8)
1 lb/500 g crabmeat
1 tablespoon fish sauce
$^1/_4$ cup/2 fl oz/60 ml coconut cream
$^1/_2$ teaspoon black pepper
$^1/_2$ cup/1 oz/30 g minced coriander with roots
3 eggs, separated
Garnish:
lettuce leaves

1. Grease six $3^1/_2$ inch/8.5 cm ramekins; set aside.

2. Heat 3 tablespoons of the oil in a wok or frying pan, until a haze forms over it. Add the shallots and garlic and stir-fry briefly until pale gold.

3. Stir in the curry paste and cook 1 minute. Transfer the mixture to a bowl.

4. Add the crabmeat, fish sauce, coconut cream, pepper and coriander and mix gently but thoroughly.

5. Beat the egg whites in another bowl until they form stiff peaks. Fold into the crab mixture.

6. Spoon the crab mixture into greased ramekins.

7. Beat the egg yolks until thick and spoon over the top of the crab.

8. Bring water to the boil in the bottom of a steamer. Place the ramekins on the steamer rack. Cover and steam over boiling water for 15 minutes. Unmould the cakes and set aside to cool and drain.

9. Heat the remaining oil and fry the crab cakes until light brown. Serve on lettuce leaves.

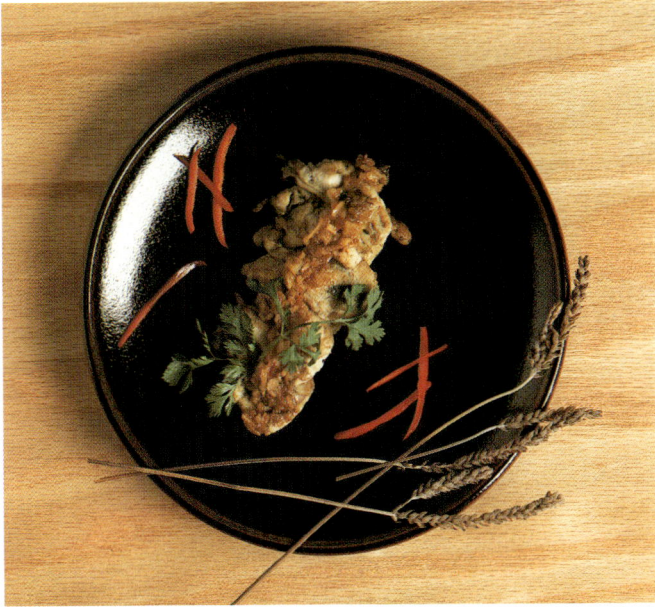

HOI NANG ROM PHAT PRIK
(RED CURRY PASTE OYSTERS)

Serves 4

2 x 8 oz/250 g jars medium oysters, rinsed and drained,
or 1 lb/500 g fresh oyster meat
2 tablespoons vegetable oil
1 inch/2.5 cm piece fresh ginger, peeled and finely chopped
3 garlic cloves, peeled and finely chopped
1 tablespoon Red Curry Paste (page 8)
1 teaspoon prawn powder
2 tablespoons fish sauce
2 teaspoons sugar
1 tablespoon lime juice
Garnish:
4 serrano chillies, thinly sliced
coriander sprigs
steamed rice

1. In a dry wok or frying pan, cook the oysters until the edges begin to curl and they begin to plump. Drain and discard liquid. Transfer the oysters to a serving plate and rinse out the wok.

2. Heat the oil and stir-fry the ginger and garlic for 2 minutes.

3. Reduce heat to low and add the curry paste. Cook for 2 minutes.

4. Meanwhile, combine the prawn powder, fish sauce, sugar and lime juice. Add the mixture to the pan with the curry paste and continue stirring for a minute more.

5. Spoon the sauce over the oysters. Garnish with chillies and coriander sprigs. Serve at once with rice.

GANG PET GUNG
(CHILLI PRAWNS)

Serves 4–6

2 lb/1 kg medium to large prawns, peeled and deveined
2 teaspoons salt
1 tablespoon chopped garlic
2 teaspoons sugar
1 tablespoon fish sauce
2 tablespoons prawn powder
$^1/_4$ cup/2 fl oz/60 ml vegetable oil
$2^1/_2$ tablespoons Red Curry Paste (page 8)
Garnish:
4 red chillies, stemmed and cut lengthwise into fine strips
lime wedges

1. Sprinkle the prawns with the salt and mix with garlic. Let marinate for 15 minutes to an hour.

2. Combine the sugar, fish sauce and prawn powder; set aside.

3. Heat the oil in a wok or frying pan until a light haze forms on the surface. Stir-fry the prawns until pink but not quite cooked through, about 2–3 minutes. Push the prawns to the outer edges of the pan.

4. Fry the Red Curry Paste for a minute or so in the centre of the pan.

5. Add the sugar, fish sauce and prawn powder, and toss the prawns evenly with the seasoning paste. Cook for 1 minute.

6. Transfer to a serving plate and strew chilli strips over the top. Serve with lime wedges.

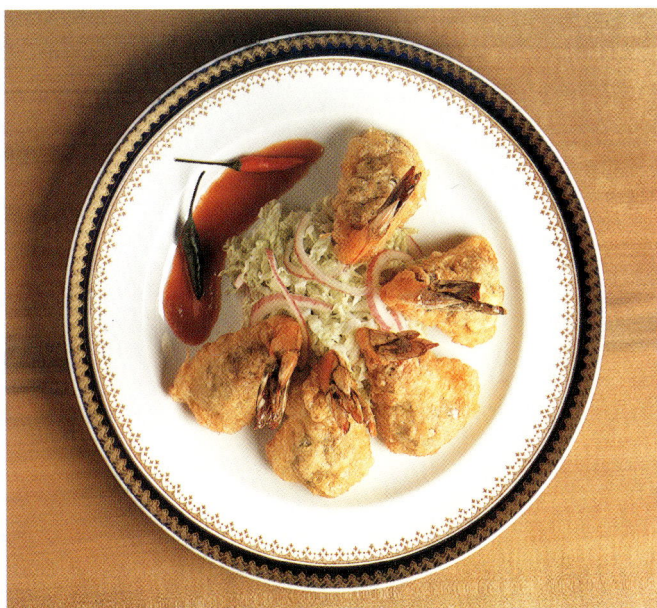

GUNG SOD SAI
(STUFFED PRAWNS)

Serves 4–6

1 lb/500 g large prawns
$^1/_4$ cup/1 oz/30 g rice flour or cornflour
10 sprigs coriander with roots
3 garlic cloves, peeled
1 tablespoon fish sauce
1 teaspoon sugar
1 teaspoon Red Curry Paste (page 8)
$^1/_2$ raw chicken breast, skinned and finely chopped
5 oz/150 g ground (minced) pork
2 eggs, beaten
$^1/_3$ cup/$2^1/_2$ fl oz/80 ml vegetable oil

1. Shell, devein and butterfly each prawn. Dip the cut side in rice flour or cornflour and shake off excess (this will help the stuffing to stick to the prawns). Reserve the remaining flour.

2. Combine the coriander, garlic, fish sauce, sugar and curry paste in a mini-processor and grind to a paste. Combine the paste with the chicken and pork.

3. Place a teaspoon or so of the stuffing mixture on each prawn, spreading it the length of the prawn with a butter knife.

4. Dust with rice flour or cornflour and coat with beaten egg.

5. Heat the oil to medium in a wok or frying pan. Fry the prawns in batches filling side up, basting continually with the hot oil, until golden, about 3–4 minutes. Transfer to a platter and serve at once.

GUNG KRATIEM
(GARLIC PRAWNS)

Serves 4–6

1 small bunch coriander with roots
3 serrano chillies, stemmed
1 head (about 13 cloves) garlic or to taste, peeled
vegetable oil, if needed
$1/4$ cup/2 fl oz/60 ml fish sauce
juice of $1/2$ lime
1 teaspoon sugar
3 tablespoons vegetable oil
$1^1/2$ lb/750 g large prawns, about 16–20, peeled and deveined
steamed rice

1. Combine the coriander, chillies and garlic in a mini-processor and grind to a paste, adding a little vegetable oil if necessary for grinding. Set aside.

2. Combine the fish sauce, lime juice and sugar, stirring to dissolve the sugar. Set aside.

3. Heat the oil in a wok or frying pan. Add the coriander paste and stir-fry until fragrant, about 1 minute.

4. Add the prawns to the wok and stir-fry, coating them with the paste, for about 2 minutes or until pink and opaque.

5. Add the fish sauce mixture and stir through.

6. Transfer to a serving plate. Serve with rice.

TORD MUN GUNG
(FRIED PRAWN CAKES)

Serves 4–6

1$^1/_2$ lb/750 g prawns, peeled and deveined
a handful of coriander sprigs with roots
6 garlic cloves, peeled
$^1/_2$ teaspoon black pepper
2 serrano chillies, stemmed
$^1/_2$ teaspoon salt or to taste
3 tablespoons to $^3/_4$ cup/6 fl oz/175 ml vegetable oil
Chilli-lime Sauce (page 19)

1. Combine all ingredients except the oil and chilli-lime sauce in a food processor and grind to a paste.

2. Wet hands and form mixture into walnut-size balls, then flatten into patties.

3. The patties may be either deep-fried in the larger quantity of oil or sautéed in a few tablespoons of oil. Heat the oil in a wok or frying pan and fry the patties in batches, turning once, until brown; avoid overcrowding. Drain on paper towels and serve with chilli-lime sauce.

GUNG YANG SOM OR
(GRILLED PRAWNS WITH CHILLI-GRAPEFRUIT SAUCE)

Serves 4–6

4 tablespoons chopped garlic
1 tablespoon Prawn Paste (page 15)
2 tablespoons fish sauce
2 teaspoons sugar
5 red chillies, stemmed and thinly sliced
2 cups Chinese cabbage, cut crosswise in 1 inch/2.5 cm pieces,
or fresh green beans, cut into 1 inch/2.5 cm lengths
4 cups/1 qt/1 l boiling salted water
4 grapefruit, peeled
2 lb/1 kg large prawns, peeled and deveined
1 teaspoon salt
1 tablespoon vegetable oil
Garnish:
coriander sprigs

1. Place 3 tablespoons of the garlic, the prawn paste, fish sauce, sugar and chillies in a serving bowl (reserve the remaining garlic).

2. Blanch the cabbage or beans in another bowl by covering it with the boiling salted water. Let stand for 1 minute and drain well.

3. Transfer the cabbage to the serving bowl with the garlic mixture.

4. Remove the membranes from the grapefruit, saving the juice. Add the grapefruit and juice to the cabbage mixture.

5. Cut each prawn in half lengthwise, then crosswise. Place in a bowl. Sprinkle with the salt and mix with the reserved garlic.

6. Sauté the prawn quickly in hot oil until just pink, no more than 1 minute.

7. Toss with the other ingredients and serve warm, garnished with coriander sprigs.

DOM YOM HOY MAN PU
(CLAMS OR MUSSELS IN CURRY PASTE BROTH)

Serves 4–6

1 tablespoon vegetable oil
2 serrano chillies, stemmed and thinly sliced
1 large shallot, chopped
4 garlic cloves, chopped
2 teaspoons Red Curry Paste (page 8) or Green Curry Paste (page 9)
2 tablespoons minced coriander
juice of 1 lime
1 tablespoon fish sauce
$^1/_2$ teaspoon sugar
$^1/_2$ cup/4 fl oz/125 ml chicken stock
2 dozen clams or mussels
steamed rice

1. Heat a wok. Add the oil and swirl until the sides are coated.

2. Combine the chillies, the shallot, garlic and curry paste and stir-fry until fragrant, about 10 seconds.

3. Add the coriander, lime juice, fish sauce, sugar and chicken stock to the wok and bring to the boil.

4. Add the clams or mussels. Cover and cook until the shells open, about 3–5 minutes. Serve hot with rice.

HOY MAN PU PRIK
(MUSSELS WITH COCONUT CHILLI PASTE)

Serves 4–6

36 large mussels, scrubbed
$^1/_2$ cup/4 fl oz/125 ml rice wine or white wine
5 fresh red chillies, stemmed, or 5 dried red chillies, stemmed,
soaked until soft in warm water and drained
2 tablespoons fish sauce
1 teaspoon palm or brown sugar
1 teaspoon Prawn Paste (page 15)
2 shallots or $^1/_2$ medium-size red onion, quartered
1 stalk lemon grass, white part only, coarsely chopped (or 1 teaspoon powdered)
1 cup/8 fl oz/250 ml coconut cream
steamed rice or French bread

1. Place the mussels in a saucepan with the wine. Cover and bring to the boil. Cook the mussels open, about 3 minutes; discard any that do not open. Remove from heat and reserve $^1/_2$ cup/4 fl oz/125 ml of the cooking liquid. Discard the top shells. Remove and discard beards. Pry each mussel loose from bottom shell, then replace it in the shell. Arrange the mussels on a serving dish and set aside.

2. Combine the chillies, fish sauce, sugar, prawn paste, shallots and lemon grass in a mini-processor and grind to a paste with the reserved mussel cooking liquid.

3. Combine the chilli paste liquid and the coconut cream in a saucepan and bring to the boil. Cook until reduced by about half.

4. Spoon the sauce over the mussels, filling the shells.* Pass the remaining sauce in a sauceboat. Serve with rice or crusty French bread.

*The mussels may be prepared ahead to this point. When ready to serve, place them on an ovenproof plate and run them under the grill or about 4 inches/10 cm from the heat source until the sauce begins to bubble.

HOY MAN PU TORD
(MUSSEL PANCAKES)

Serves 4–6

12–16 mussels, scrubbed
3 tablespoons cornflour
3 tablespoons rice flour
$^3/_4$ teaspoon salt
2 eggs, lightly beaten
1 tablespoon minced garlic
3 tablespoons chopped coriander leaves
1 tablespoon chopped spring (green) onion
2 tablespoons vegetable oil
black pepper
coriander sprigs, lime wedges and 1 cup bean sprouts for garnish
Sriracha Sauce (page 20)

1. Bring the mussels to boil in 1 cup/8 fl oz/250 ml water. As soon as the shells open, remove the meat; discard any mussels that do not open. Discard the beards and shells. Strain the cooking liquid and let cool.

2. Mix the cornflour, rice flour and salt. Stir in the beaten eggs. Add the mussel cooking liquid and stir until smooth.

3. Fold the garlic, coriander, spring onion and mussel meat into the egg mixture.

4. Pour half the oil into a wok or 9 inch/23 cm frying pan, tilting and swirling the oil so that the bottom and sides are thoroughly coated.

5. Ladle half the mussel batter into the pan. When the pancake has set slightly, lift its edges to let the batter run into the pan. Cover and cook slowly until the top is almost dry.

6. Loosen the pancake with a wooden spatula. Cover the pan with a slightly larger plate and invert the pancake onto the plate. Slide the pancake back into the frying pan uncooked side down and cook another 2–3 minutes. Slide the pancake onto a serving platter.

7. Repeat with the remaining oil and batter.

8. Sprinkle the pancakes with pepper. Garnish with coriander, lime wedges and bean sprouts. Serve with Sriracha sauce.

HOY MAN PU DOON
(THAI STEAMED CLAMS OR MUSSELS)

Serves 4–6

24–36 medium clams or mussels, scrubbed
3 tablespoons fish sauce
1 teaspoon sugar
4 serrano chillies (2 red, 2 green), stemmed, seeded and finely chopped
4 garlic cloves, finely chopped
juice of 1 lime
Garnish:
basil leaves

1. Place the clams in a saucepan with $^1/_2$ cup/4 fl oz/125 ml water. Cover, turn the heat to high and steam them until they open, 2–4 minutes. Divide the clams among individual serving bowls. Strain the stock, reserving $^1/_3$ cup/$2^1/_2$ fl oz/80 ml.

2. Combine the fish sauce, sugar, chillies, garlic, lime juice and reserved clam stock.

3. Ladle the stock over the clams. Strew with basil leaves and serve hot.

MU MAKEUA
(PORK WITH AUBERGINE AND BASIL)

Serves 6–8

6 serrano chillies
6 garlic cloves, peeled
1 medium-size yellow onion, quartered
2 lb/1 kg Japanese or Thai aubergine
3 cups/24 fl oz/750 mg water
2 teaspoons salt
scant ¼ cup/2 fl oz/60 ml vegetable oil
1½ lb/750 g lean pork, cut into 2 x ¼ inch/5 x 5 mm strips, or
1 lb/500 g ground (minced) pork
¼ cup/2 fl oz/60 ml fish sauce
2 tablespoons soy sauce and 2 teaspoons sugar
¼ cup/2 fl oz/60 ml water
1 cup/2 oz/30 g basil leaves
steamed rice

1. Combine the chillies, garlic and onion in a mini-processor and grind to a paste. Set aside.

2. Remove the stem ends of the aubergines. Cut aubergines in half lengthwise, then cut crosswise into 2 inch/5 cm pieces.

3. Bring the water and salt to a boil in a wok or frying pan and parboil the aubergine pieces 2–3 minutes. Drain. Dry the wok thoroughly with a paper towel.

4. Heat the wok for 2 minutes or until the rim is hot. Add the oil and heat until a slight haze forms on the surface. Add aubergine and stir-fry for about 5 minutes or until lightly browned and slightly shrivelled, turning frequently (the aubergine will reduce in volume by at least half). Remove from the wok with a slotted spoon and drain on paper towels. Transfer to a serving plate or bowl.

5. Stir-fry the onion paste until golden, about 5 minutes.

6. Add the pork and stir-fry until it loses its pinkness and is cooked through, about 3–4 minutes.

7. Stir in the fish sauce, soy sauce and sugar and mix well.

8. Add the water and bring to the boil. Stir in the basil leaves. Spoon the mixture over the aubergine and mix thoroughly but gently. Serve with rice.

MU PAD PRIK SOD
(PORK WITH CHILLIES)

Serves 6

2 lb/1 kg lean pork
1 tablespoon cornflour
2 serrano chillies
2 yellow chillies
2 red jalapeño chillies
3 tablespoons vegetable oil
2 shallots, sliced
6 garlic cloves, chopped
3 tablespoons fish sauce
2 teaspoons sugar
steamed rice

1. Cut the pork against the grain into $^1/_4$ inch/5 mm slices. Cut the slices into 2 inch/5 cm squares. Place in a bowl.

2. Sprinkle the pork with the cornflour and work it through thoroughly.

3. Remove the stems from the chillies, and slice them lengthwise into slivers. Set aside.

4. Heat the oil in a wok, swirling to coat the sides. Stir-fry the shallots and garlic until golden, about 3 minutes.

5. Add the pork and toss until it begins to brown, about 4 minutes.

6. Meanwhile, mix the fish sauce and sugar, stirring to dissolve the sugar. Add to the wok and stir through. Cook until the liquid is almost absorbed, about 2 minutes. Serve with rice.

MA HO
(ORANGE SLICES TOPPED WITH PORK)

Serves 6–8

4 navel oranges, peeled and cut into $^1/_4$ inch/5 mm slices
2 tablespoons vegetable oil
6 garlic cloves, chopped
2 shallots or $^1/_2$ medium-size red onion, chopped
$^1/_3$ cup/2 oz/60 g chopped roasted peanuts
1 teaspoon Prawn Paste (page 15)
2 serrano chillies, stemmed and sliced crosswise
1 lb/500 g ground (minced) pork
$^1/_2$ teaspoon salt
$^1/_2$ teaspoon sugar
1 teaspoon black pepper
Garnish:
mint leaves

1. Arrange the orange slices on a serving platter.

2. Heat the oil in a wok, swirling to coat the sides. Stir-fry the garlic and shallots until golden, about 3 minutes.

3. Add the peanuts, prawn paste and chillies. Toss to coat with the oil.

4. Add the pork, salt, sugar and pepper. Break up the clumps of pork and stir-fry until it is cooked, about 4–5 minutes.

5. Mound the pork on the orange slices and garnish with mint leaves. Serve warm or chilled.

MU KRATIEM PRIK
(GARLIC PEPPER PORK)

Serves 6

2 lb/1 kg lean boneless pork*
1 head garlic, peeled (about 13 cloves)
$^1/_2$ cup/2 oz/60 g coriander roots
3 tablespoons fish sauce
4 teaspoons freshly ground white pepper
3 tablespoons vegetable oil
steamed rice
Chilli-lime sauce (page 19)

1. Slice the pork against the grain into $^1/_4$ inch/5 mm slices; cut the slices into 2 inch/5 cm squares. Set aside.

2. Combine the garlic, coriander, fish sauce and pepper in a mini-processor and grind to a paste. Set aside.

3. Heat the oil in a wok, swirling to coat the sides. Stir-fry the paste for 2 minutes over medium heat.

4. Add the pork to the wok and mix with the paste. Turn the heat to high and stir-fry the pork until it starts to brown, about 4 minutes. Serve with rice and chilli-lime sauce.

*Or substitute calves' liver, cut the same way.

MU TANG
(GROUND PORK AND PRAWNS IN COCONUT CREAM)

Serves 4–6

8 fl oz/250 ml coconut cream
$^1/_4$ cup/1 oz/30 g minced coriander roots
6 garlic cloves, minced
2 tablespoons fish sauce
1 teaspoon sugar
$^1/_2$ teaspoon white pepper
12 oz/350 g ground (minced) pork
12 oz/350 g raw prawns, shelled, deveined and minced
2 red chillies, thinly sliced
Rice Crusts (page 105)

1. Place half the coconut milk in a wok and boil over high heat until thickened, about 15 minutes.

2. Add the coriander root, garlic, fish sauce, sugar and pepper to the thickened coconut cream and mix well.

3. Stir in the pork and cook until it loses its pinkness.

4. Add the prawns, red chillies and remaining coconut cream and bring to the boil. Reduce heat and simmer about 5 minutes. Serve over rice crusts.

TORD MUN NUA
(THAI MEATBALLS)

Serves 4–6

$^1/_2$ head garlic (about 7 cloves), peeled
$^1/_2$ medium-size yellow onion, peeled and halved
2 tablespoons chopped coriander with roots
1 tablespoon fish sauce
1 tablespoon soy sauce
1 teaspoon black pepper
$^1/_2$ teaspoon nutmeg
12 oz/350 g ground (minced) beef
12 oz/350 g ground (minced) pork
1 large egg, beaten
$^1/_2$ cup/2 oz/60 g plain flour*
$^1/_2$–$^3/_4$ cup/4–6 fl oz/125–175 ml vegetable oil*
Chilli-garlic Sauce (page 17) or Sriracha Sauce (page 20)

1. Combine the garlic, onion, coriander, fish sauce, soy sauce, pepper and nutmeg in a mini-processor and grind to a paste.

2. Place the beef, pork and egg in a mixing bowl. Add the paste and mix well.

3. Form the mixture into meatballs about 1 inch/2.5 cm in diameter.

4. Coat with flour and deep-fry in hot oil until brown.* Serve hot with chilli-garlic sauce or Sriracha sauce.

*If desired, omit step 4; form the meat into patties and grill or fry.

MU KRATIEM
(GARLIC PORK)

Serves 4–6

$^1/_4$ cup/1 oz/30 g coarsely chopped coriander roots
7 large garlic cloves, peeled
$^1/_2$ teaspoon salt
2 teaspoons white pepper
$1^1/_2$ lb/750 g pork steaks, about $^1/_2$ inch/1 cm thick
$^1/_3$ cup/$2^1/_2$ fl oz/80 ml vegetable oil
2 cucumbers, peeled, seeded and sliced paper thin
Chilli-lime Sauce (page 19)

1. Combine coriander roots, garlic, salt and pepper in a food processor and grind to a paste.

2. Spread the paste on both sides of the pork steaks. Cover and refrigerate overnight.

3. Heat the oil in a frying pan. Fry the pork steaks about 3 minutes on each side, or until both sides are lightly browned and the inside is cooked but moist.

4. Meanwhile, place the cucumber slices in a serving bowl.

5. When the pork is cooked, remove from pan. Stack the pieces and cut against the grain into slices about $^1/_4$ inch/5 mm thick.

6. Place the meat and its juices on top of the cucumber. Serve with chilli-lime sauce.

MU YAW
(THAI SAUSAGE)

Serves 6

2 lb/1 kg pork shoulder or butt, coarsely ground
6 garlic cloves, peeled
16 coriander roots
4 serrano chillies, stemmed
1 tablespoon salt
2 teaspoons black pepper
$2^{1}/_{2}$ tablespoons plain flour
6 x 10 inch/25 cm squares of muslin or
12 large-diameter sausage casings
Chilli-lime Sauce (page 19)

1. Place the pork in a mixing bowl.

2. Combine the garlic, coriander roots, chillies, salt and pepper in a mini-processor and grind to a paste. Scrape into the bowl with the meat.

3. Sprinkle the flour and work the paste and flour evenly through the meat.

4. Divide the mixture into 6 portions. Roll each portion into a cylinder.* Wrap each cylinder into cheesecloth, twisting the ends and tying with string. (Or stuff the meat into sausage casings, tying the ends with string and pricking each casing several times.)

5. Bring 2 inches/5 cm of water to the boil in a frying pan. Add the sausages, return to the boil and lower the heat. Cover and simmer for 30 minutes. They are ready to be eaten at this point, or you may proceed to the next step.

6. Remove the cheesecloth and fry the sausages until lightly browned. Serve hot or cold with chilli-lime sauce.

*Sausages may be steamed without cheesecloth or casings at this point.

KAI TORD GUP MU
(GROUND PORK OMELETTE WITH CHILLI-LIME SAUCE)
Serves 4–6

$^1/_4$ cup/2 fl oz/60 ml vegetable oil
4 garlic cloves, chopped
4 shallots, chopped
4 serrano chillies, stemmed and minced
8 oz/250 g lean ground (minced) pork
1 tablespoon chopped coriander
2 tablespoons fish sauce
4 eggs
Garnish:
Crisp-fried Garlic or Shallot Garnish (page 98)
or Crisp-fried Onion Garnish (page 99)
Chilli-lime Sauce (page 19)

1. Heat a wok. Add half the oil and swirl to coat the sides. Stir-fry the garlic, shallots and chillies until softened, about 1 minute.

2. Add the pork and stir-fry until no longer pink, breaking up large lumps with the back of a fork.

3. Stir in the coriander and fish sauce and mix well. Remove wok from heat. Preheat the oven to 150°F/65°C/warm.

4. Beat the eggs. Add the pork mixture and mix thoroughly.

5. Scrape and wipe out the wok. Reheat with the remaining oil, swirling to coat the sides. Ladle in a quarter of the omelette mixture (a sixth of the mixture if you are serving 6) and fry until the bottom is golden and the edges are crisp. Turn and fry the other side. Keep warm in the oven. Repeat the procedure until all the egg is cooked.

6. Serve hot garnished with fried garlic, shallots or onions. Accompany with chilli-lime sauce.

GAENG KEOWAN GAI
(GREEN CURRY CHICKEN)

Serves 4–6

3 tablespoons vegetable oil
2–3 lb/1–1.5 kg chicken, jointed
2 rounded tablespoons Green Curry Paste (page 9)
1 cup/8 fl oz/250 ml coconut cream
3 serrano chillies, stemmed and slivered
2 tablespoons fish sauce
4 kaffir lime leaves (if dried, soak in warm water for 15 minutes)
30 mint or basil leaves
steamed rice

1. Heat the oil in a wok. Add the chicken pieces and stir-fry for 5–10 minutes or until lightly browned. Remove from wok and set aside.

2. Turn the heat to medium and stir-fry the curry paste for 2–3 minutes.

3. Stir in the coconut cream and mix well. Bring to the boil and cook until the mixture thickens and reduces by about one-third, scraping up the browned bits.

4. Add the chillies, fish sauce, lime leaves and chicken pieces with their juice. Bring to the boil. Reduce heat and simmer uncovered until the chicken is cooked through, about 30 minutes.

5. Stir in the mint or basil leaves. Serve with rice.

GAENG PHET GAI
(RED CURRY CHICKEN)

Serves 4–6

1 cup/8 fl oz/250 ml coconut cream
2 tablespoons Red Curry Paste (page 8)
3 lb/1.5 kg chicken, skinned and jointed
2 tablespoons fish sauce
2 teaspoons sugar
1 large tomato, peeled and chopped
1 tablespoon tamarind water (page 115)
steamed rice

1. In a wok or saucepan large enough to hold the chicken pieces, boil the coconut cream, stirring, until slightly thickened, about 10 minutes.

2. Stir in the curry paste and cook 2 more minutes.

3. Add the chicken pieces and bring to the boil. Reduce heat to low and simmer 20–30 minutes or until the chicken is tender.

4. Add the fish sauce, sugar, tomato and tamarind water and simmer 5 minutes more. Ladle into bowls and serve with rice.

GAENG KEOWAN GUNG
(GREEN CURRY PRAWNS)

Serves 4–6

1$\frac{1}{2}$ cups/12 fl oz/350 ml coconut cream
2 tablespoons Green Curry Paste (page 9)
2 slices fresh galangal, crushed
1$\frac{1}{2}$ lb/750 kg medium prawns, peeled and deveined
2 tablespoons fish sauce
Garnish:
3 serrano chillies, stemmed and slivered lengthwise
10 basil leaves
steamed rice

1. Bring half the coconut cream to the boil in a wok or saucepan. Cook briskly until it is reduced to the consistency of thick cream, about 15 minutes.

2. Stir in the curry paste and galangal and boil for 3 more minutes, stirring frequently.

3. Add the remaining coconut cream and return to the boil.

4. Add the prawns and return the coconut cream to the boil. Reduce heat and cook 3–4 minutes or until the prawns are firm and opaque. Remove from heat.

5. Stir in the fish sauce. Transfer to a serving bowl.

6. Garnish with chillies and basil leaves and serve with steamed rice.

GAENG SOM GUNG
(PRAWNS IN SOUR CURRY)

Serves 4–6

$1^1/_2$ cups/12 fl oz/350 ml coconut cream
2 tablespoons Orange Curry Paste (page 10)
1 medium tomato, peeled, seeded and chopped
pinch of salt
pinch of sugar
$^2/_3$ cup/5 oz/150 ml water
$^3/_4$ teaspoon red chilli flakes
2 teaspoons Prawn Paste (page 15)
$^1/_2$ teaspoon tamarind concentrate or 2 tablespoons lime juice
2 tablespoons fish sauce
1 teaspoon sugar
1 lb/500 g medium to large prawns, shelled and deveined
4 courgettes (zucchini) cut into $^1/_2$ inch/1 cm rounds
basil leaves for garnish

1. Boil the coconut cream for 15 minutes or until thickened and oily around the edges.

2. Meanwhile, combine the curry paste, tomato, salt and sugar in a small bowl. Set aside.

3. Combine the water, chilli flakes, prawn paste, tamarind, fish sauce and sugar in another saucepan. Bring to the boil, breaking up lumps with a wooden spoon.

4. Add the prawns and boil 2–3 minutes or until done. Remove from stock and set aside.

5. Add the courgettes to the prawn stock and boil for 3 minutes. Remove from stock and set aside.

6. Boil the prawn stock briskly for 5 minutes to reduce. Stir into the coconut cream and return to the boil.

7. Stir in the curry paste mixture and boil gently for 5 minutes. Adjust seasonings.

8. Place equal amounts of prawn and courgette in individual serving bowls. Ladle the sauce over and garnish with basil leaves.

GAENG NUA BAI MANGLUK
(CURRIED BEEF WITH PUMPKIN AND BASIL)

Serves 4–6

2 tablespoons vegetable oil
1–2 tablespoons Red Curry Paste (page 8), depending on desired
hotness
1$^1/_2$ lb/750 g sirloin steak, sliced lengthwise into 3 inch/7.5 cm strips,
then crosswise into $^1/_8$ in/3 mm slices
2 cups/16 fl oz/500 ml coconut cream
2–3 tablespoons fish sauce
8 oz/250 g pumpkin or other hard-shelled squash, peeled and cut
into 1 inch/2.5 cm cubes
basil leaves for garnish

1. Heat the oil in a wok or saucepan over low heat and fry the curry paste until fragrant, about 3 minutes.

2. Raise the heat and add the beef, stirring to coat each slice with the curry paste.

3. Stir in the coconut cream and fish sauce and bring to the boil.

4. Add the pumpkin. Cover* and cook over low heat for 10 minutes or until the pumpkin is tender.

5. Garnish with basil leaves.

*If you are using coconut cream made with milk, do not cover the saucepan or the liquid will curdle.

GAENG KARI NUA
(YELLOW BEEF CURRY)

Serves 6

1 cup/8 fl oz/250 ml coconut cream
2 lb/1 kg sirloin steak
1 tablespoon Red Curry Paste (page 8)
1 tablespoon turmeric
3 inch/7.5 cm cinnamon stick
3 star anise
2 kaffir lime leaves (if dried, soak in warm water for 15 minutes)
2 large yellow onions, thinly sliced
steamed rice

1. Bring the coconut cream to the boil in a wok or saucepan. Reduce heat and simmer for 10 minutes or until thickened and oily around the edges.

2. Meanwhile, cut the steak lengthwise into 3 inch/7.5 cm strips, then crosswise into $1/8$ inch/3 mm slices.

3. When the coconut milk has thickened, stir in the curry paste, turmeric, cinnamon, star anise and lime leaves. Cook briskly until reduced by half.

4. Stir in the beef and onions and reduce heat to low. Simmer uncovered for 30 minutes. Serve with rice.

PANANG NUA
(PENANG BEEF)

Serves 6

2 lb/1 kg sirloin steak
1 tablespoon vegetable oil
6 kaffir lime leaves, slivered (if dried, soak in warm water for 15 minutes and drain)
3 tablespoons Penang Curry Paste (page 12)
3 tablespoons fish sauce
2 teaspoons sugar
$^{1}/_{2}$ teaspoon paprika
2 cups/16 fl oz/500 ml coconut cream
3 tablespoons ground roasted peanuts
about $^{1}/_{3}$ cup/$2^{1}/_{2}$ fl oz/80 ml chicken stock
Garnish:
2 serrano chillies, stemmed and cut lengthwise into slivers
30 basil leaves

1. Cut the sirloin steak lengthwise into strips 3 inches/7.5 cm wide. Cut each strip crosswise into $^{1}/_{8}$ –$^{1}/_{4}$ inch/3–5 mm slices.

2. Heat the oil in a wok and stir-fry the beef until no longer pink. Remove and wipe out the wok.

3. Combine the lime leaves with the curry paste, fish sauce, sugar and paprika. Set aside.

4. Boil the coconut cream in a wok or saucepan until thickened to the consistency of sour cream.

5. Stir in the curry paste mixture, peanuts and beef. Cook at high heat for 2–3 minutes, adding chicken stock as necessary if the mixture becomes too thick. Transfer to a serving bowl.

6. Garnish with chillies and basil leaves.

GAENG PHET MU MAKEUA
(PORK AND AUBERGINE CURRY WITH BASIL)

Serves 6

2 cups/16 fl oz/500 ml coconut cream
2 tablespoons Red Curry Paste (page 8)
2 lb/1 kg lean pork, cut into 2 x $^1/_8$ inch/5 cm x 3 mm strips
6 Japanese or Thai aubergines, stemmed and cut into $^1/_2$ inch/1 cm rounds
2 kaffir lime leaves, slivered (if dried, soak in warm water for 15 minutes)
3 red chillies, stemmed, seeded and slivered
3 green chillies, stemmed, seeded and slivered
3 tablespoons fish sauce
1 teaspoon sugar
Garnish:
basil leaves

1. Heat $^1/_4$ cup/2 fl oz/60 ml of the coconut cream in a wok or saucepan. Stir in the curry paste and cook 2 minutes or until fragrant.

2. Add the pork and cook 2–3 minutes, stirring to coat with the sauce.

3. Add the remaining coconut cream with the aubergine, lime leaves and chillies and cook over medium heat until the coconut cream is oily and thickened and the aubergine is tender but not mushy, about 10 minutes.

4. Add the fish sauce and sugar, stirring to dissolve the sugar.

5. Transfer to a serving bowl and garnish with basil leaves.

GAENG PED MU
(COUNTRY-STYLE PORK AND VEGETABLE CURRY)

Serves 6

1 cup/4 oz/125 g Chinese cabbage, cut crosswise into 1 inch/2.5 cm
slices
1 cup/4 oz/125 g green beans or Chinese long beans, cut into 2 inch/5 cm
lengths
$^1/_2$ cup/2 oz/60 g peeled and thinly sliced Japanese white radish
(daikon)
2 tablespoons vegetable oil
1 tablespoon Red Curry Paste (page 8)
2 lb/1 kg lean pork, cut into 2 x $^1/_2$ inch/5 cm x 5 mm strips
3 tablespoons fish sauce
1 teaspoon tamarind concentrate
1 teaspoon sugar
Garnish:
4 red or green serrano chillies, seeded and slivered
10 basil leaves
steamed rice

1. Soak the cabbage, beans and daikon in ice water for 30 minutes.
Drain well.

2. Heat the oil to medium in a wok or frying pan. Stir in the curry
paste and cook until fragrant, about 1 minute.

3. Stir in the pork, coating the pieces evenly with the paste.

4. Add the cabbage, beans, daikon and chillies to the wok and stir-fry
for 2 minutes.

5. Stir in the fish sauce, tamarind and sugar. Cover and simmer for 7
minutes.

6. Garnish with chillies and basil and serve with rice.

GANG KEOWAN PET
(DUCK CURRY)

Serves 6

1 cup/8 fl oz/250 ml coconut cream
2 tablespoons Green Curry Paste (page 9)
1 duckling (about 3 lb/1.5 kg), skinned and cut into serving pieces
(reserve skin for cracklings*)
3 tablespoons fish sauce
1 cup/8 fl oz/250 ml chicken stock
5 kaffir lime leaves (if dried, soak in warm water for 15 minutes)
2 serrano chillies, stemmed, seeded and slivered
Garnish:
10 basil leaves
duck cracklings
steamed rice

1. Place $^1/_4$ cup/2 fl oz/60 ml of the coconut cream in a wok or frying pan and turn heat to medium. Stir in the curry paste and cook until fragrant, about 1 minute.

2. Add the remaining coconut cream and cook briskly until slightly thickened and oily.

3. Add the duck pieces and reduce heat.

4. Stir in the fish sauce, chicken stock, lime leaves and chillies. Cover and cook over low heat until the duck is tender, about 30–40 minutes.

5. Skim off the fat and adjust the seasonings. Transfer to a serving bowl.

6. Garnish with basil leaves and cracklings. Serve with rice.

*Cut the duck skin into $^1/_4$ inch/5 mm strips and fry in a frying pan until crisp and brown. Reserve for garnish.

PAD THAI
(THAI FRIED NOODLES)

Serves 4

3 tablespoons fish sauce
$1/4$ cup/2 fl oz/60 ml white distilled vinegar
2 teaspoons sugar
$1^1/2$ tablespoons tomato paste
$1/3$–$1/2$ cup/$2^1/2$–4 fl oz/80–125 ml vegetable oil
1 tablespoon chopped garlic
$1/3$ cup/2 oz/60 g each raw prawns, chicken and pork, cut into bite-
size pieces or 1 cup/6 oz/175 g prawns, shelled and deveined
3 hanks rice vermicelli or bean thread noodles, soaked in warm water
for 15 minutes and drained
2 eggs
1 cup/4 oz/125 g bean sprouts
4 spring (green) onions, sliced diagonally into 1 inch/2.5 cm pieces
Garnish: $1/2$ teaspoon red chilli flakes, chopped coriander leaves,
1 tablespoon prawn powder, 2 tablespoons chopped peanut and 1 lime

1. Combine the fish sauce, vinegar, sugar and tomato paste. Set aside.

2. Heat $1/3$ cup/$2^1/2$ fl oz/80 ml oil in a wok or frying pan. Add the garlic and fry gently until golden.

3. Add the prawns, chicken and pork and stir-fry 2 minutes.

4. Add the noodles to the pan and toss lightly.

5. Pour the fish sauce mixture over the noodles and toss gently until thoroughly coated.

6. Break one of the eggs into a small bowl. Add a bit more oil to the wok if it seems necessary. With a spatula, lift up the noodles on one side and slide the egg underneath, breaking the yolk. Repeat the process on the other side of the wok with the remaining egg. Let cook undisturbed for 4 minutes or until eggs are set.

7. Sprinkle on the bean sprouts and spring onions.

8. Gently fold the eggs into the noodles by scooping underneath the noodles and folding the mixture over. The noodles are fragile at this point and care should be taken not to break them.

9. Transfer the noodles to a serving plate. Strew with chilli flakes, coriander, prawn powder and peanuts. Surround with lime slices and serve immediately.

BA MEE TOOA
(SPICY PEANUT NOODLES)

Serves 4–6

1 tablespoon chunky peanut butter
juice of $\frac{1}{2}$ lime
2 tablespoons sesame oil
$\frac{1}{4}$ cup/2 fl oz/60 ml fish sauce
2 tablespoons soy sauce
$\frac{1}{2}$ teaspoon sugar
1 tablespoon chopped garlic
$\frac{1}{4}$–$\frac{1}{2}$ teaspoon red chilli flakes
1 tablespoon prawn powder
1 lb/500 g angel hair or vermicelli noodles, cooked according to
package directions and drained
6 spring (green) onions, cut diagonally into $\frac{1}{2}$ inch/1 cm pieces
8 oz/250 g cooked prawns, shelled and deveined
3 red serrano chillies, stemmed and thinly sliced
Garnish:
$\frac{1}{3}$ cup/2 oz/60 g peanuts, coarsely ground
Crisp-fried Onion Garnish (page 99) or Crisp-fried Shallot Garnish (page
98)
coriander sprigs

1. Combine the peanut butter, lime juice, sesame oil, fish sauce, soy
sauce, sugar, garlic, chilli flakes and prawn powder.

2. Place the noodles in a serving bowl and toss with the peanut
butter mixture.

3. Strew with spring onions, prawns and red chillies.

4. Garnish with peanuts, fried onions and coriander sprigs. Serve at
once.

WOON SEN GUNG
(TRANSLUCENT NOODLES WITH LIME PRAWNS)

Serves 4–6

4 oz/125 g bean thread noodles, soaked in tepid water for 15 minutes
12 oz/350 g prawns, shelled and deveined
juice of 1 lime
$1/2$ cup/2 oz/60 g dried prawns, coarsely chopped
$1/4$ cup/2 fl oz/60 ml fish sauce
1 teaspoon sugar
2 celery stalks, julienned
4 spring (green) onions, cut diagonally into $1/2$ inch/1 cm pieces
Garnish:
coriander sprigs
red chillies, stemmed and thinly sliced

1. Place the soaked noodles in a strainer and dip in boiling water for 2 seconds, then plunge into ice water. Drain well. Snip them in half with scissors, then in half again. Set aside.

2. Cook the prawns in boiling water for 1 minute or just until opaque. Drain.

3. In a serving bowl, toss the cooked prawns with the lime juice. Let marinate for 15 minutes.

4. Add the dried prawns, fish sauce and sugar and mix well.

5. Add the celery, bean threads and spring onions and toss through.

6. Garnish with coriander and chillies. Serve at once.

KANOM JIN SAUHAM
(NOODLES WITH COCONUT CREAM AND GINGER)

Serves 4–6

1 lb/500 g rice or wheat vermicelli
$^1/_3$ cup/$2^1/_2$ fl oz/80 ml fish sauce
$2^1/_2$ teaspoons sugar
juice of 1 lime
6 garlic cloves, chopped
1 cup/4 oz/125 g dried prawns, rinsed, drained and finely chopped
$^1/_2$ cup/2 oz/60 g peeled julienned fresh ginger*
2 red chillies, stemmed and chopped
2 green chillies, stemmed and chopped
1 cup/6 oz/175 g fresh pineapple, peeled and chopped
1 cup/8 fl oz/250 ml coconut cream, heated

1. Cook the vermicelli according to package directions. Plunge into tepid water to stop the cooking. Drain.

2. Place in a serving bowl and toss with the remaining ingredients. Serve hot or warm.

*Use less ginger if you prefer a milder dish.

MEE BAI MANGBOK
(THAI NOODLES WITH BASIL)

Serves 4–6

1 lb/500 g Thai egg noodles or linguine
2 tablespoons vegetable oil
8 garlic cloves, chopped
2 tablespoons fish sauce
$^{1}/_{4}$ cup/2 fl oz/60 ml chicken stock
1 teaspoon soy sauce
1 cup/2 oz/60 g basil or spinach leaves
$^{1}/_{2}$ teaspoon white pepper
Garnish:
2 red serrano chillies, stemmed and thinly sliced

1. Cook the noodles according to package directions. Drain.

2. Heat the oil in a wok or frying pan and sauté the garlic until golden.

3. Add the drained noodles and stir to coat.

4. Add the fish sauce, stock, soy sauce, basil and pepper. Simmer for 3–4 minutes, stirring gently so as not to break the noodles.

5. Transfer noodles to a serving bowl and garnish with chillies. Serve hot.

KAO MUN
(RICE COOKED IN COCONUT CREAM)

Makes 3–4 cups

1 cup/7 oz/200 g long-grain rice, washed until the water runs clear
1 teaspoon salt
2 cups/16 fl oz/500 ml coconut cream
4 garlic cloves, finely chopped
2 shallots, finely chopped
Garnish:
1 cup/6 oz/175 g shredded fresh pineapple
Crisp-fried Garlic or Shallot Garnish (page 98),
or Crisp-fried Onion Garnish (page 99)

1. Combine the rice, salt, coconut cream, garlic and shallots in a pot large enough to allow the rice to triple in volume.

2. Cover and bring to the boil over high heat. Lift the lid briefly and stir to loosen any rice that may have stuck to the pot. Cover again immediately and simmer *without stirring or lifting the lid* for 20 minutes. Let stand, covered, for 5 minutes. Transfer to a serving bowl.

3. Garnish with pineapple and fried garlic, shallots or onions and serve at once.

TORD KRATIEM
(CRISP-FRIED GARLIC OR SHALLOT GARNISH)

Makes about ²/₃ cup/3 oz/85 g

Fried garlic and shallots are sold in jars or plastic bags in many Asian markets.

1 cup/8 fl oz/250 ml vegetable oil
1 cup/4 oz/125 g chopped garlic or shallots

1. Heat the oil to moderate. Add the garlic and fry slowly, stirring frequently, until golden.

2. Immediately remove from heat and let the garlic brown in the hot oil.

3. Drain well, reserving the flavoured oil for future use. This will keep for a month or so in a closed container in the refrigerator.

HUA HOM TORD
(CRISP-FRIED ONION GARNISH)

Makes about 2 cups/12 oz/350 g

5 medium to large red onions
1 cup/8 fl oz/250 ml vegetable oil

1. Cut the root ends off the onions. Cut them in half, then in half again into quarters. Slice the quarters into thin slivers. Transfer to a bowl and separate the layers.

2. Heat half the oil in a wok or frying pan. Add half the onions, tossing to coat each sliver with oil. Stir-fry until nearly crisp, watching constantly so that the onions don't burn and become bitter. Remove from heat and allow the onions to brown in the oil. Drain on paper towels.

3. Repeat the process with the remaining oil and onions. Store in a plastic container in the refrigerator.

KAI KEM
(SALTED EGGS)

These eggs are handy to have around as a garnish or as a surprise ingredient in salads. Use as you would unsalted hard-boiled eggs. They look lovely on the shelf in glass jars and make interesting gifts.

1 cup/8 oz/250 g salt
4 qt/4 l water
1 dozen eggs in shells

1. Combine the salt and water and bring to the boil. Stir to dissolve the salt. Let cool.

2. Carefully arrange the uncooked eggs in a jar or crock, being careful not to crack the shells.

3. Pour the salted water over the eggs. Cover and let stand 30 days to allow the salt to penetrate the yolks.

4. Hard-boil in the normal fashion before using.

KAI LUK KUI
(SWEET AND SOUR HARD-BOILED EGGS)

Serves 8

This makes a nice light lunch or an interesting tart-sweet side dish.

2 tablespoons fish sauce
2 teaspoons Sriracha Sauce (page 20)
$1/4$ cup/2 oz/60 g palm or brown sugar
3 tablespoons tamarind water (page 115) or vinegar
$1/2$ cup/4 fl oz/125 ml water
$1/3$ cup/$2^1/2$ fl oz/80 ml vegetable oil
8 hard-boiled eggs, shelled
$1/2$ cup/3 oz/85 g Crisp-fried Onion Garnish (page 99)
$1/2$ cup/3 oz/85 g Crisp-fried Garlic Garnish (page 98)
Garnish:
4 fresh red chillies, stemmed, seeded and slivered
coriander sprigs

1. Combine the fish sauce, Sriracha sauce, sugar, tamarind water and water in a pot and bring to the boil. Cook until thickened, about 10 minutes. Set aside.

2. Heat the oil. Add the eggs and stir-fry until they are blistered and brown. Transfer to a serving plate and slice in half lengthwise.

3. Spoon the sauce over the eggs and strew with fried onion and garlic. Serve hot, garnished with slivered chillies and coriander sprigs.

KAI DOON
(STEAMED EGGS)

Serves 4–6

8–10 large eggs, beaten
3 shallots, finely chopped
3 garlic cloves, finely chopped
3 spring (green) onions, thinly sliced
3 serrano chillies, stemmed and thinly sliced
3 tablespoons fish sauce
$^1/_2$ teaspoon white pepper
$^1/_2$ cup/4 oz/125 g ground (minced) pork or coarsely chopped raw prawns
$^1/_2$ cup/4 fl oz/125 ml chicken stock
1 teaspoon vegetable oil
steamed rice

1. Combine all ingredients except the oil.

2. Use the oil to thoroughly grease the bottom and sides of a flat-bottomed heatproof casserole dish that is at least 1 inch/2.5 cm smaller in diameter than the steamer.

3. Pour the egg mixture into the casserole and place in the steamer. Bring the water in the bottom of the steamer to the boil. Cover and steam the eggs for 15–20 minutes or until set.

4. Serve hot with rice.

TANG KWA AJAD
(CUCUMBER CONDIMENT WITH CHILLI)

Makes about 1³/₄ cups/14 oz/400 g

Serve this chilled with curries and fried foods. Make it fresh each time; it does not hold up well.

2–3 cucumbers, peeled, seeded and sliced paper thin
1 medium-size red onion, sliced paper thin
³/₄ teaspoon salt
2 teaspoons sugar
3 tablespoons rice vinegar
3 serrano chillies, stemmed and sliced paper thin
2 tablespoons coarsely ground peanuts

1. Place the cucumber and the onion in a serving bowl.

2. Combine the remaining ingredients except the peanuts, stirring to dissolve the sugar and salt.

3. Pour over the cucumber and onion and toss well.

4. Sprinkle with peanuts just before serving.

HUA HOM SOD SAI
(PORK AND CRABMEAT-STUFFED ONIONS)

Serves 6

12 oz/350 g ground (minced) pork
12 oz/350 g crabmeat
6 garlic cloves, finely chopped
2 teaspoons black pepper
10 coriander sprigs with roots, finely chopped
1 tablespoon vegetable oil
2 tablespoons fish sauce
1 teaspoon sugar
6 white or yellow onions, peeled and steamed for 5 minutes
Chilli-lime Sauce (page 19) or Sriracha Sauce (page 20)

1. Place the pork and crabmeat in a bowl.

2. Add the garlic, pepper and coriander and mix through.

3. Heat the oil in a frying pan or wok. Stir-fry the pork mixture until the pork is no longer pink, about 4 minutes.

4. Add the fish sauce and sugar and remove from heat.

5. Cut the bottoms from the onions so they stand straight. Scoop out the centres, leaving the shell about $^1/_2$ inch/1 cm thick. Save the centres for another use, or discard.

6. Pack the filling into the shells. Set the onions on a plate at least 1 inch/2.5 cm smaller in diameter than the steamer rack. Steam until the onions are tender, about 12 minutes. Serve with chilli-lime sauce or Sriracha sauce.

KAO TUNG
(RICE CRUSTS)

A great use for leftover rice. Serve with curries, soups or ground-meat dishes such as Ground Pork and Prawns in Coconut Cream (page 77) and Ground Pork and Tomato Sauce (page 13).

1. Spread the thinnest possible layer of cooked rice on an ungreased baking sheet.

2. Bake at 150°F/65°C/warm for several hours until crisp. (Or allow to air-dry for a week or two.)

3. The crust may be broken into chunks and served as is, or fried in vegetable oil until golden and drained on paper towels.

KANOM MO KANG
(COCONUT CUSTARD)

Serves 6

1 teaspoon vegetable oil
1 cup/8 fl oz/250 ml coconut cream
$^{1}/_{2}$ cup/4 oz/125 g light brown sugar
$^{1}/_{2}$ teaspoon salt
2 tablespoons rum
2 teaspoons orange liqueur
6 eggs, beaten.

1. Preheat oven to 350°F/180°C/Gas 4. Coat a 9 inch/23 cm square baking pan with the vegetable oil.

2. Combine the coconut cream, sugar, salt, rum and liqueur. Whisk in the eggs.

3. In a double saucepan over medium heat, whisk the mixture constantly until it thickens and becomes slightly curdy, about 7 minutes.

4. Pour the egg mixture into the prepared pan and bake about 30 minutes or until firm.

5. Run under a griller until golden brown. Cut into squares. Serve warm or at room temperature.

KLUAY BWARCHEE
(BANANAS IN COCONUT CREAM)

Serves 4–6

6 green bananas, peeled and cut into rounds 1 inch/2.5 cm thick
1 cup/8 fl oz/250 ml coconut cream
1 teaspoon orange flower water (optional)
$^1/_2$ cup/4 oz/125 g palm or brown sugar
pinch of salt
Garnish:
1 teaspoon cinnamon

1. Combine all ingredients except garnish in a saucepan and bring to a rolling boil.

2. Reduce heat and simmer 5 minutes.

3. Place in a serving bowl and sprinkle with cinnamon. Serve hot.

KLUAY TORD
(FRIED BANANAS)

Serves 4–6

2 large eggs, beaten
$^1/_4$ cup/2 oz/60 g palm or brown sugar
$^3/_4$ cup/3 oz/85 g rice flour
$^1/_4$ cup/1 oz/30 g shredded coconut
$^1/_4$ cup/2 fl oz/60 ml ice water
4–6 firm, ripe bananas
$^1/_4$ cup/2 fl oz/60 ml vegetable oil or 2 tablespoons butter or
margarine

1. Mix the eggs thoroughly with the brown sugar.

2. Add the rice flour, coconut and ice water and mix well.

3. Peel the bananas. Cut in half lengthwise, then in half crosswise. Dip each quarter in the batter and coat thoroughly.

4. Heat the oil. Saute bananas until crisp and brown, turning once. Drain on paper towels. Serve immediately.

MANGO DAIQUIRIS

Serves 4

$^1/_2$ cup/4 fl oz/125 ml light or dark rum
$1^1/_2$ cups/12 oz/350 g mango pulp (about 2 large mangoes)
$^1/_4$ cup/2 fl oz/60 ml simple syrup*
juice of 1 lime
2 cups/8 oz/250 g ice cubes
Garnish:
mint sprigs

1. Purée the rum, mango, syrup and lime juice in a blender.

2. With the motor running, add ice cubes two at a time until the mixture is slushy.

3. Serve at once, garnished with mint sprigs.

*For simple syrup: In a saucepan, combine $^1/_2$ cup/4 oz/125 g sugar and 1 cup/8 fl oz/250 ml water and bring to the boil, stirring constantly until sugar is completely dissolved. Cool. Store at room temperature in a tightly covered container. Makes about 1 cup/8 fl oz/250 ml.

POTENT PINEAPPLE PUNCH

Serves 8

juice of 2 limes
1 cup/8 fl oz/250 ml simple syrup (see recipe for Mango Daiquiris, page 109)
$^1/_2$ cup/4 fl oz/125 ml light or dark rum
$^1/_4$ cup/2 fl oz/60 ml gin
$^1/_4$ cup/2 fl oz/60 ml Mekong whisky or bourbon
$^1/_4$ cup/2 fl oz/60 ml grenadine or maraschino cherry juice
1 cup/8 fl oz/250 ml pineapple juice or ginger ale
ice cubes
Garnish:
1 pineapple, peeled and chopped
maraschino cherries
mint sprigs

1. Combine the liquid ingredients and ice cubes in a punch bowl.

2. Garnish with the fruit and mint sprigs.

NAM CHA
(THAI ICED TEA)

Serves 4

1 cup/8 fl oz/250 ml sweetened condensed milk
1 tablespoon simple syrup (see recipe for Mango Daiquiris, page 109),
optional
2 cups/16 fl oz/500 ml strong warm Thai tea
shaved ice
1 cup/8 fl oz/250 ml light cream

1. Add the sweetened condensed milk and the simple syrup to the warm tea and mix well. Let cool to room temperature.

2. Just before serving, fill tall glasses with shaved ice. Half-fill the glasses with the tea mixture.

3. Top up the glasses with light cream and swirl with a spoon.

GLOSSARY

Anise: Available as a whole or powdered pale green seed or as a dark brown star-shaped pod (star anise) with a strong licorice flavour and aroma. It is used to flavour both sweet and savoury dishes.

Aubergine: The Japanese or Thai aubergine is very different in texture to the familiar western vegetable. There are several forms and most will prove difficult to find outside Southeast Asia. The most common of these are like baby green tomatoes. Common eggplant or fresh peas can be substituted depending on the recipe but the flavour will be markedly different.

Bamboo shoots: A pale yellow vegetable, the young shoots of the bamboo plant, frequently used in oriental cooking. Readily available in cans.

Banana leaves: Used as a lining for moulds, or for wrapping meats and fish for steaming. Available in oriental and Hispanic markets.

Basil: An aromatic leafy plant with a faint licorice fragrance. Thais use many varieties of basil, among them "holy" basil and lemon basil. The common green variety is perfectly adequate. It is used in curry preparations, salads and stir-fry recipes. Sold in most markets.

Bean curd (*tofu*): Processed from soybeans, tofu is a smooth, custardy product high in protein. It is sold in slabs and is readily available at oriental and local markets.

Bean paste: Usually made from soybeans and chillies to which garlic and sugar and sometimes added. Readily available in jars in oriental markets.

Bean sprouts: Sprouted mung beans. Readily available at local and oriental markets.

Bean threads (*saifun*): Translucent noodles made of mung bean starch. They are sold dried in cellophane packages and must be soaked in water before use.

Chillies (*prik*): Thais use many varieties of chillies, dried and fresh. Tiny red bird chillies, about an inch (2.5 cm) long, are used in sauces and curries (bright green Mexican serrano chillies may be substituted). Japalenos, also Mexican in origin, are used in some recipes. These are slightly larger and plumper than the serrano with a blackish green skin and are extremely hot. They are usually pickled in brine or canned. Chillies are fiery hot and care should be exercised in handling them; as with all chillies, *always* wash your hands with soap and water afterward, and *never* rub your eyes if your hands have chilli oils on them. Chillies keep for several weeks if kept dry, wrapped in a paper towel and stored in the refrigerator. They are available in most markets.

Coconut milk and cream: Unsweetened coconut cream, a rich, thick substance used in curries and other Thai recipes, is sold in cans in markets that cater to an oriental and Filipino clientele. To prepare coconut milk and cream from scratch, scrape the meat from a fresh coconut; discard the shell. Cut the flesh into 1 inch/2.5 cm chunks. Grate by hand or in a food processor (or start with unsweetened desiccated coconut sold commercially in bags).

For cream: Cover 1 cup/8 fl oz/250 ml of grated coconut (fresh or packaged) with 1 cup/8 fl oz/250 ml boiling water or milk for each cup of coconut. Let stand for 30 minutes, then squeeze through muslin or a clean dishcloth to extract the liquid.

For milk: After the first squeezing of the coconut to extract the cream, cover the grated coconut once again with 1 cup/8 fl oz/250 ml boiling water or milk. Proceed as above. (The second and third pressings of the coconut flesh give a thinner, less oily liquid.)

Refrigerated, coconut cream and coconut milk will keep for the same length of time as dairy milk. Frozen in plastic bags, they will keep indefinitely.

Coriander: (Mexican or Chinese parsley, sometimes called cilantro). The flavour of the coriander leaf does not resemble that of its seed, which is used in most curries. The whole plant – roots, leaves, stems and seeds – is used in Thai cooking. Coriander is very perishable. It keeps longest when rinsed, shaken dry and stored in the refrigerator in a covered container. Mint, parsley and basil are, on limited occasions, fairly adequate substitutes.

Curry leaves: Small, aromatic leaves that resemble bay leaves. Available in packages in oriental markets.

Curry paste: All manner of pastes are available for nominal prices in Thai, Filipino, Indian, Vietnamese and other specialty markets. Recipes for making your own are in the Sauces and Condiments chapter.

Daikon (also known as **great white radish** or *mooli***):** This versatile vegetable is widely used in Asian cuisine. It is similar in taste to tender young turnip which can be used as a substitute.

Dried prawns: Readily available in oriental and Hispanic markets. Prawns must be soaked in hot water for 15 minutes or so before using.

Fish sauce (*nam pla*): Also called fish soy and fish gravy. A thin, salty, amber-coloured liquid extracted from fermented anchovies or prawns. This potent-smelling condiment is to Thai food what soy sauce is to Japanese and Chinese cuisine. Readily available in most oriental markets. Filipino *patis*, Burmese *ngan pya ye* and Vietnamese *nuoc mam* are good substitutes.

Five spice powder: This is the best-known of Chinese spice blends and is a rich, aromatic mixture of star anise, fagera, cassia or cinnamon, cloves and fennel seeds. It is available ready mixed at most supermarket spice counters.

Galangal (*kha, ka* or *laos*): A tuberous member of the ginger family, which it resembles in shape. Also sold in powdered form. One teaspoon powder equals one $^1/_4$ inch/5 mm slice. To keep fresh galangal, peel, slice and store in a plastic bag in the freezer. May be found in Indonesian, Thai and most other oriental markets.

Garnishes: Thais used fried garlic (page 98), fried onions (page 99), thinly sliced spring (green) onions, red or green chillies, coriander sprigs, thinly sliced cucumber or limes, red chilli flowers and spring onion brushes (see below).

To make chilli flowers: Cut the tip off the chilli. Holding the chilli pepper by the stem, cut toward the stem end, stopping almost at the base. Continue to cut thin parallel strips about $^1/_{16}$ – $^1/_{18}$ inch/2-4 mm wide. Place the chilli in ice water and the strips will separate into petals and curl like a flower.

To make spring onion brushes: Cut off the root end of a spring onion. Cut off the dark green leaves at the point where they form a single stalk. You should be left with a piece about 3 inches/7.5 cm long. The green end will be the handle and the white end the brush. With a needle or pin, start a slit 1 inch/2.5 cm from the green end (handle) and slit all the way down through the white bulb at the end (brush). Rotate the onion a quarter turn and repeat the process. Continue rotating, making your slits as close to one another as possible. Place the spring onions in ice water to hasten the curling of the white leaves.

Fried garlic and fried onions: Sold in plastic containers or jars in oriental markets. To make them from scratch, see pages 98 and 99.

Ginger: A knobby root with tan skin and yellow, fibrous flesh. Readily available in local and oriental markets. Peel, slice and freeze it in a plastic bag, or chop it in a food processor and store in an airtight jar covered with vegetable oil. It will keep for months in the refrigerator. If kept dry, wrapped in a paper towel and refrigerated, the root will keep for several weeks. Powdered ginger is not a substitute.

Kaffir lime (*makrut*): The fresh fruit is pear-shaped with a bumpy, wrinkled rind. Both the leaves and the peel are used in gravies and curry pastes. Sold fresh, dried and frozen in oriental markets. Regular lime rind and citrus leaves are an adequate substitute.

Laos powder: See Galangal.

Lemon grass: Sold in Thai markets as *serai.* An elongated grey-green spring onion-shaped plant of the citronella family, having a bulbous tip and fibrous leaves. It is also sold in powdered and flake form. The powder may be used without soaking; the dried flakes must be soaked first. One teaspoon dried equals one stalk of lemon grass. Dried lemon peel is a fairly adequate substitute.

Light cream: Single cream.

Noodles: Are second to rice in importance in a Thai meal. They are made from a variety of flours, among them wheat, rice and mung beans.

Palm sugar: Also known as jaggery. A soft, brown, caramel-flavoured sugar from the sap of the coconut palm. Brown sugar may be substituted.

Pomelo: A citrus fruit resembling a large grapefruit, but with fewer membranes.

Prawns, dried: See Dried prawns.

Prawns, prawn paste (*kapi* or *kapee*): A salty, potent paste made from pounded prawns and salt. Available in cans or jars in oriental markets, labelled *bagoong* in Philippine markets. Anchovy paste is a good substitute, but halve the amount. Because of its high salt content, *kapi* does not require refrigeration. See recipe on page 15.

Prawns, powder: A pungent seasoning made by crushing dried prawns with a pestle and mortar to form a fine powder.

Rice flour: A powder made of finely ground white rice. Used for the making of noodles and pastry and as a thickener. Stores indefinitely without refrigeration. Available in oriental markets.

Rice sticks: Dried white translucent noodles, made of rice, used for soups and in the preparation of *pad thai.* They require soaking in cold water for 15 minutes before using.

Shallots: A bulbous member of the onion family often referred to as "Bombay onion". It is a hard small onion with a reddish-brown tough skin. The Thai version is smaller than our domestic shallot. Red onion is a good substitute.

Soy sauce: Infrequently used in Thailand. Instead, fish sauce (*nam pla*) is used in much the same manner.

Sriracha sauce: A commercially made, ready-to-use hot chilli sauce made with serrano chillies, vinegar, garlic, salt and sugar. It is the ketchup of Thailand, though a fiery version, and is available in markets catering to Thai and Vietnamese clientele (see page 20 for recipe).

Star anise: See Anise.

Straw mushrooms: A stemless, globe-shaped mushroom the size of a quail's egg with a distinct earthy taste. Fresh straw mushrooms are rarely available and they do not keep well. The canned variety is readily available in oriental markets.

Sweet basil: See Basil.

Tamarind: A fuzzy brown pod resembling a dried lima bean. The pulp is used to give a sour taste to soups and sauces. Tamarind paste is sold in brick form or in jars in oriental markets.

To make tamarind water: soak 1 tablespoon tamarind pulp in warm water for about 5 minutes, mashing the pulp well with the back of a fork to dissolve it. Lemon or lime juice is a fairly adequate substitute.

Tendons: Sinewy white ligaments sold in meat markets that cater to an Asian clientele.

Tofu: See Bean curd.

Turmeric: A member of the ginger family, turmeric is used throughout Asia for its musky flavour and attractive golden colour (not unlike saffron). Mostly used in powdered form, it is available fresh in some Asian shops in the West and one teaspoon of powder equals 1/4 inch/ 5 mm slice.

INDEX

Fitsum Melaku

Domestic Solid Waste Management